BOOKS BY ROBERT KELLY

LAPIS

POEMS BY

ROBERT KELLY

A BLACK SPARROW BOOK
DAVID R. GODINE · *Publisher* · *Boston*

This is
A Black Sparrow Book
published in 2005 by
David R. Godine, Publisher
Post Office Box 450
Jaffrey, New Hampshire 03452
www.blacksparrowbooks.com

Author's Note: These poems were composed from 1997 through 2001. Some of
them have been published in *Barrow Street*, *Conjunctions*, *First Intensity*, and
Poets & Writers. The images by Matisse refer to the great wall drawings in the
Chapel at Vence. "In Provence" is dedicated to Esther Sobin; her father, the poet
Gustaf Sobin, was my host during a week among the sunflowers and lavender.
The French phrase in "Good Friday 1997" means "it shone on Jesus and his
mother." "The View from Michigan Avenue" wanders through the great collec-
tions of the Museum of the Art Institute of Chicago one winter afternoon.

Book design and composition by Carl W. Scarbrough

The Black Sparrow Books pressmark is by Julian Waters
www.waterslettering.com

Library of Congress Cataloging-in-Publication Data
Kelly, Robert, 1935–
Lapis : poems / by Robert Kelly.—1st ed.
p.   cm.
"A black sparrow book."
ISBN 1-57423-186-3 (Paperback)
I. Title.
PS3521.E4322L37   2005
811'.54—dc22
2004016724

First Edition
Printed in Canada

for Charlotte

CONTENTS

7

8

9

LAPIS

THREE EXPLANATIONS

ESSENCES

The essences are here.
Matisse traces a dove
with charcoal on big paper
and suddenly it's white,

traces St Dominic, traces
an archangel looking curiously
down the south of France,
Matisse walks in sandals

over the classified ads of papers
neatly spread out on the floor,
his feet on paper move, his hand
holds the long drawing wand

and traces through the air some
plain and fancy holy people
and a dove to carry the earth to us
as it did in the days of Noah

in its vastly strong and fragile beak.

SNOW ON THE SANGRE DE CRISTOS

How could I know I would never
be in 1954 again,
eat Camembert in the Luxembourg?
How could I know

even the war would leave me?
I was a broken bridge,
a burning vineyard, a rock
beneath a waterfall,

an empty bottle, a hold-up man
dead outside a convenience store.
We were not born
for gondolas,

the church never forgives us,
the mail never comes.
We went one morning
to the sanctuary of Chumayó

where sick people eat holy mud.
We thought of eating it,
and the thought was enough to cure
since our malady was mind.

THE ANNALIST

Sometimes I wish I were Pepys or John Evelyn
or Gilbert White, nothing to do but write down
the weather of the world and men's opinions.

And maybe that is all I do, here
in this transparent cipher of my verse.
Tell how deep the snow fell,

the lawn how wet, then dream of seed.
Or go to town and dine with busy men
who tell their dreams

masquerading as politics and fact.
We all are dreamers on a deedless earth.

FOUR PORTRAITS

JOHN DILLINGER

In the shallow night of summer
lakes we are fugitives
from no man's justice
hiding from the women in red

until at length
we weary of concealment
and go back to Mickey Mouse
and welcome the bullet

(it has my name on it).
To die in a glamorous alley
in the rain (it was not
raining) is an exquisite

poetry, isolate
from doctors and attorneys;
to die alone with love,
with the beautiful enemy

watching scared policemen dance.

EMILY DICKINSON

Are we allowed to think she masturbated,
that some of her poems trace
sure as spiderwebs the spread
of who she was and what she wanted

and what it felt like to be her,
grace or grudge, in a world
by love infected but in a place
all too rescued from the scarlet plague,

the hilltop forts of conscience and the Mind
stretching like Mount Tom above a snowy
landscape shot through with evening sun
turning everything red but her skin pale?

EDITH WHARTON

Buy some something for someone
that is it. The transaction

is all that matters. A bread,
a cake. Pour tea on the floor

pour milk in her lap.
The giving is what counts.

Pour. Gaze in her eyes
while you pour the cream,

she heaps sugar in your lap
with a silver spoon.

Metals are important.
People are sticky. Time

is about being together,
there is no other reason for a day,

a week. Keep looking
in her eyes. Between

the two of you
is everything you have ever

seen. That means all there is.
There is no place

you have not been.
Now slice the cake

many slices
more than you need

make her take
one in each hand.

You forgot the butter
she says. You are sorry

there is no butter.
Nothing but me

and you. We have to be
yellow together,

we have to spread
greasily over things

so the house
will remember us

you say. She still
would like some butter

but she is quiet.
Nothing is perfect

the tea is good.
Strong because forgotten

in the teapot while
all the pouring went on,

the laps, the eyes, the pause
that never stops being

an interruption even after
you are talking again.

Everything is fine.
I like the cake, she says.

I like what we are doing
to each other. The sun

is going down, what we say
might be important,

very. You are glad
she said that, very.

It is important
to be polite, to give

every person what she wants.
The only morality

is to make people happy,
you both know that,

you say nothing.
You tell about a book

you dreamed finding
and dreamed reading.

She listens to you
as if it were a real book,

as if you wrote it,
the story you tell.

Someone wrote it,
she says, that is only

reasonable, it is there,
you tell it, it must

have been you
she says. No, no, you say,

trying to explain
and understand at once.

She smiles at you
and wants more tea.

This time you pour
and see her eyes again,

the tea overflows
the cup the saucer

also is lapping over its edges
more mess more sweet

confusion. Sugar, she heaps
one in the cup and one

on you. The sacrament
is eternal, we believe

in bread and milk.
We touch each other

and leave traces
you say. Or she says,

it is no longer important
which mouth says it.

Or even what it says.

WILLIAM BUTLER YEATS

For three years Yeats and I
were together in this world.
The room was small.
I heard him breathing.

A wild today I walked
on the hill, the highland
by the river, and came home
exalted weary from the wind;

now I cannot hear my leg,
I know it's there, I turn
this way and that and cannot hear
the feel of it. I get up

and come to the table. Yeats is gone,
the coffee still warm. Listen,
great wind of earthly springtime,
I feel something. It must finally be me.

MATURITY

I was a child in a world with no children
so I took the measure of adults
and became one.

But the adult I am is an eight-year-old grown-up,
unchanged, fixed in the amber of my childhood ardor,

the lust to know everything
and touch everyone everywhere

which is what I supposed adults were able to do,
to eat what they want and travel from country to country

and not stand bent to the ground
like the old man who kept chickens on Avenue R.

GOOD FRIDAY 1997

It is the hour when he starts his climb.
It's like going to the market or the mall,
carrying all at once every item

you have ever bought or stolen. The weight
of all our merchandise is his cross.
He carries what we want.

Stumbles under the deadweight of our desires,
falls. The crowd in the galleries of the mall
jest or sympathize and look away.

Nothing can be done. Once the process
has begun there is no end until the end.
How can he do what he's doing?

No one can carry all the things we want
and yet he does. A hundred-pound sack of potatoes
from Hoople, North Dakota. A three-piece lounge suite

(loveseat, armchair, ottoman) in blue satin,
an oxcart with a broken wheel, the Venus of Praxiteles,
the works of Walter Scott, he holds them all

and then he falls. Simon of Cyrene stands there
till a cop tells him to lend a hand, why not,
he likes all this stuff, he hoists it on his back,

trudges ahead of Jesus up the shallow hill.
In this story the sun is always shining.
Il avait lui sur Jésus et sa mère,

it shone on Pilate and on Tiberius,
spring calm over Mare Nostrum. Jesus
empty-shouldered now falls one more time

but the gospels are not watching. He sprawls
on cobblestones, his mouth near wet rock,
he whispers what a road knows how to hear,

now any road on earth can say it,
you can hear it if you just kneel down,
put your warm cheek to the ground and listen.

MOONSET

After dying there is not much reason,
mostly just remembering. Flags hang loose
and the wind is somewhere else.

What is sleep here is war in heaven.
And hell is broken in its boundaries,
the naked Queen of Love comes down the stairs

and leads her lover back — this is the Moon
setting every night — one at a time
all the dead gods come back

as us. And all the while the son of god
battles sodden sleepers there, breaks
the patterns of their thinking, wakes them

into mild discontent with how things are.
From which a resolution slowly grows
to have done with clinging and with dying.

By an immense window, her silhouette
tells you what you need to know
and we are rinsed into the sky.

TOMB IN THE GARDEN

It is the third day
counting from never.
You know that heaven's close

because the soldiers are asleep
and stone rolls itself away
and a man tells a woman not to touch him —

I would die for your touch,
I think, you Madeleine,
and yet my hands shrink back,

I say I am risen, I am another.
I am no more the man you think.
No more the man I too once thought,

I am but I am not. If you try
to touch me you would be appalled
by the silence of my skin.

For this absence burns like fire —
the kind of fire you only half-see
on a match tip in the noontime sun,

a flame no flame, a quivering absence
in the air. If you touched me all the air
would flee from you, my touch

would stifle you, all the oxygen you are
would burn in that empty fire
to make me into something you can see.

AN ANCESTOR WHO FOUGHT
AT GETTYSBURG

The conditions of human warfare are always barbaric,
he said, lifting the martini rather faster than was prudent
south or north. Have you had one three or wine? I asked,
and realized my own condition left something to be desired.
More wine. More light. When I was a child we knew
a family with a crazy old man in the attic; he had a silver
plate (they told me) in his head, and raved around at night
swinging his old sword. Yes, he had been in the War
of Northern Aggression. And no, I don't know whether
in fact he fought at Gettysburg. All I knew was another man
with another sword in his hand chopped a hole in his head
and the silver plate (they explained to me) was to keep
his brain from rushing out. I wondered if it tarnished
since all I knew of silver was Saturday night spent burnishing
mother's wedding flatware. Christ, it is so stupid to be young.

VENTADORN:
Can vei l'auzeta mover

I will go to places
where once the lark
rose on the astonished wind
and women listened hard
as men tried to hear out loud
the intelligence of that bird

who from the passing
of kind upon kind
knew all and knows all
our days will know
to take his little love
high into the absolute air.

A WEAVER

If I were a weaver I would have a bird to carry
one line lightquick beneath another then over
until each articulation wound itself forever
round every other and the thick world sang.

But I am no kind of dancer, you hear my breathing
heavy as a hammer nailing shades to shadows,
birdless trying to negotiate each silver absence
into the semblance of something someone said.

And who is the mother of that conversation,
the original intelligence of which these yawps
are tender echoes? Trying to tell you,

trying to tell you true. We walk in cities
remembering the woods — all we can hope
is to liberate the blessed opposite in things.

A CONCERTO OF
ERNEST CHAUSSON

all our sense of music
bleak-thorned a vague moon
tangled in branches hot
breath of a spring night
your throat cooled by what it says

forgives the living
their fitful loves,
forgives us for forgetting
the needy dead,

           the Unity
flows around us, midnight blooming jessamine
and over the soft waves of the lake
well-heeled convalescents at Montreux
hear the sobbing of Pontius Pilate
under the interminable years.

THE RETURN

Among old shoes in someone's vestibule
wonder if any of them are ours

did we come here once before
before they lit the moon one night
and before the sea was filled?

This dust in the corner was my mother,
this dead mouse by my boot tip
was the golden monarch of Lahore.
Before I even get my coat off
I am scared of the place that's come to me

again, a trick time plays on me over and over,
no way to win when time has *da capo* in his hand.
Even before I open the screen door

to hail all my dumb Irish in the kitchen
loud and proud palavering and embrace
in some detail their horny sisters,
the kick of rage unwinds my chest,

I know I'm falling for it all again,
squeeze and smooch and paramour

while all outside live cleanly in the dark
bluets, and little bats, and pimpernel.

ADORNO ON SIBELIUS

Dürftig, the man said, needy, feeble, leaving
much to be desired. I like the word. I like a world
that needs me, a dance that has room for me
to take the floor, take my partner by the hips
and whirl ourselves into that benign confusion
solemn personages study all their weary lives
and identify as Culture, Civilization, Art.
We know what it is, it is a waltz, quick rap,
cartoon of a long-eared jackass smeared on plaster,
it is Rome and pederasty and a marble god
broken at the house door while we slept. It is war.
It is Strauss: the last trio of *Der Rosenkavalier* —
when love is gone then everything is gone.
Just sand and oil wells stretching to the burnt
horizon. Distance is the neediest art of all.

IN PROVENCE

And as for the holy,
let us be that too.

Elderberry, weasel
running soft across the road,
a snake with legs and fur,

I contradict myself
because I speak. Elder,
or any other flower,

even that one
that smells so rich
like jasmine, in moonlight
it looks red, just across
from the little town hall,

the other
meaning of any
flower is silence.

SABOTAGE

For years we drove by that ruined river.
Now the phlox has faded, the tiger
lilies that cruised the road a month ago
are few, and faded, like the paltry
horde of Mongols left when Genghis died
and all that host resorbed into its genesis.
Sabotage. Time's work. O woe,
the years have vanished all my hue,
I who once was bronze-beard and a bear.

2.

But still I know the mulchy pathways of the wood,
where the viper crosses, where the springs are
that deep in drought make muddy footsteps here,
I still know how to listen to the leaves. And higher
and further than any tree, the vagrant
wisdom of the crows. They talk through me
when I have the sense to listen. Sabotage
means poetry. Changing what the world
naturally speaks.

3.

Or we are nature's way
to change her name. To speak a new word.
I think I heard it in the cloisters of Provence
where monks in incomprehensible silences
austerely strolled, squaring every circle,
round gardens shouting with scarlet flowers,
men who had chosen to hide from the world
and now had the world at their feet,
lavender, and stock, and marigold, and fatal oleander.

THE QUIZ

Years ago, when my father would come home from work, I used to ask him for something. If he wasn't too tired. I'd ask him to ask me questions. Years before that, before the war, he used to bring me home a little toy most nights, little leaden animals, realistic, smooth to the touch, truly colored, little animals from Germany and France. Crocodile, giraffe, eland, lion, tiger, ostrich, beaver, stag. They were the people I lived most closely with all day, and little tin soldiers from Saxony. Then the war came, and I grew older, and no father keeps bringing presents, and there was my little sister now, an infant, sweet and well-behaved and pale. But still whenever my father came home I'd ask him something. I'd ask him to ask me questions.

Give me a quiz, Daddy — that was the formula with which I would open negotiations. Some nights it happened. Some nights he would smile and begin to ask me some questions. There were never enough, they were never hard enough, but they were questions, and I lived to answer them.

I loved being asked questions — data, mostly, of course, state capitals, history, science, any fact at all — I didn't worry yet about what a fact was. And yet there already was a strange, half-lit, early evening, tree-shadowed kind of doubt in me about the world that questions tried to touch, and from which answers came.

At night, when the sky comes close at first, the world closes in around us. All the lovely distances turn grey and shrivel up. In just such an hour once I called for my quiz, and my father paused before he answered by asking.

My father paused. We were under the plane trees whose scabby bark made all kinds of disease seem close. Diseases mentioned in the Bible. The air was very warm still, and bats plunged in and out of the streetlights. We were not walking, we were standing still in front of the synagogue. Was he thinking of a question? Or was he deciding whether or not to ask a question already formed in his mind? While he was considering, bats were skimming through the heavy air, and moths began to bother the streetlights they would besiege all night long. Trees rustled in the nice little land

37

breeze that stirred up every night, air shifting from the island to the nearby sea. The leaves lifted all together and fell back.

My father paused and suddenly I felt full of a weird hollow kind of terror. Anticipation, certainty, dread. Some part of me knew what was coming. Something was coming, some terrible thing. It would be the worst question in the world — the answer would rise up in me and blast me. I could feel the question coming, and the answer waiting. Waiting inside me. The terrible thing was inside me waiting to come out. I did not want to hear myself think, because even thinking about the shape of where the answer was waiting filled me with terror; the answer itself would destroy me. I could feel the hot breath of the answer eager to speak into my empty, empty brain. I had asked for the question, and the Wrong Question would come, the one that called for the Right Answer. The worst issues I could think of, the things I always feared and dreaded: leopards, leprosy, the god who lives in hell, the old man who ate some strange wheat and turned into stone, the dusty dolls beneath the old bed — all of them were implicit in the answer, yet even those, which I could almost bear the pain of thinking, which I could almost already hear thinking — even those were not the worst. It was something else.

After that day I asked him for no more questions.

Now you're the one who has to ask me. Please.

Questions unlock the hell in which all the lost answers broil and seethe. Someday the answers, even *that* answer, must speak themselves into the astounded air. It may be the last thing I will ever hear.

You should live so long, the man said, listening to my rant. *Go out and feed the birds*, he said, *buy some seed. All you know how to do is talk to stones, and plant milk in the ground.*

THE LOST CHORD

There was a song they sang before I was young
before I even went to confession
and sometimes the old ones sang it still:

*Seated one day at the organ   I was weary and ill at ease   and my
fingers wandered idly   over the noisy keys   is what I remember,
then I heard what sounded like: I know not what I was playing   or
what I was dreaming of   when I struck one chord of   music
something more   like the sound   of a   grand Amen   like the
sound   of a   grand   A   men.*

    Heavy with rubato the song went on, vaguely praising and
despairing, never being able to hear that chord again. "The Lost
Chord," they called it.

    It spoke of the impossibility of the merely possible. Surely
there is a finite number, even if it is very large, of chords that human
hands can play at an organ, however many manuals the organ
might have. Ten fingers. Finite. Of course that chord. Could be found.
And played. Again. Ten fingers will always win. Of course they could
find it, but the mind can never come to that place again. The fingers
can find the chord but not the resonance. Never again the mood or
mind or moot or mum or means or mark or murk or mild or muss
of whatever images they were that dragged along through the slug-
gish sarabande of consciousness while the fingers played.

    What was the man at the organ dreaming? His wife's breasts
or the fulvous marmot sunning itself on the path up to Montriond
or the face on his mother's sleep when she was just a few hours this
side of dying. Her last face. Or just a streak of dust on a window
pane in the light of rain. Or nothing but the pale pleasant snoozy
somnolence of not paying attention to what your hands are doing?
Ten fingers. Of course the chord, though all its notes and registers
be found, will never be found. Its resonance in mind is long, though.
Whatever happens lasts a long time. And even what we feel casts a
shadow, and in the shade of feeling we go on living. Ten fingers and

one mind, all the vibrant images lost on the heave or spurt or swoon of orgasm. All the lost imaginings. All the vanished doors.

All music starts in reverie — didn't Plato warn us, Lydia's lewd modal dissolution leaching our sobriety? How can a republic stand up against the fantasy of its citizens?

> Because we hide our fantasies from one another
> We can be ruled by politics and priests and war.

She looked closely at me and asked what logic entitled me to say that. I said No logic, or The logic of oranges and lavender and south wind — that's what poetry comes from, and what it devours.

No logic (I went on, growing confident) but the logic of the Secret Alphabet, the hidden firmament behind the sky, the eternally proliferating sculpture of light and warmth and turbulence through which we move all our lives and never look at, never see. Stare into boiling water and see the endlessness of art, the changefulness of beauty. It is movement, it all is movement. It is nothing but movement observed and cherished, lovingly observed and understood. Let the kettle be your study in its rolling boil. Watch the wind rise.

Yes, yes, she said, I know all that. I have lived amongst you all of my life, and I have seen your waters boil. But logic I was demanding, and you have none, no logic at all. You are not entitled to what you said about Fantasy and War.

I didn't say it. The words said it. Words say themselves, and we just listen out loud. I'm just the shabby dusty city park they play in. Poor words, to have me for their only greenwood!

You may hear them all you please, but you have no right to let the words out, she said, no right at all. Unless you study them alertly;

then, if what they say conforms to what you yourself believe or trust or practice, then you may speak them with sincerity.

I believe nothing, trust nothing, and have no practice but listening to them speak through me.

Let them speak, but you have no right to repeat, to me and to others, what you fancy you hear the words saying.

On the contrary, I have no right to impede their passage. I am a road, a crossroads, trivial, glorious. Three peasants on their way to a dance walk right through me, queens sail by in their palanquins, the shadows of hanged men swaying on their gibbet fall across me. I am a road, not a judge, not a philosopher. I am a road. I am a door.

Only one man ever is a door. She said this sadly, and I wanted to cheer her up:

We all are him. Or he is me, I, who am speaking to you now, am he.

She shrieked and held her soft hands over her ears. (I wanted to be her hands.) You're nobody, she said, nobody. Or maybe you yourself are the terrible answer to the unasked question. Maybe your father meant to ask you *Who will you be?* And from the agony and horror of the future, your answer spoke: *I will be me.* And nothing after that, just a door swinging open and slamming shut in the desert wind.

FOREIGNER

Have you ever felt like a foreigner
in your own body, as if your hipbone
spoke Spanish and wanted to dance?

Have you ever awakened to hear
your bones counting themselves,
saying Touch me, touch me?

Have you ever felt like a cornfield
in a drought, or an empty canoe
going down the rapids, or as if all

your uncles and aunts are impostors
and you were born on the wrong planet?

Have you ever opened the newspaper
and found a dead animal or a piece
of moldy bread? Have you ever

felt that the kitchen door is a doctor
and he's watching you?

DECISION

1.

There is some sort of decision brewing. A hand
holding a cap up to the sky as if the stars are coins
and one will fall. Take this. Spend it on difference.
Make change where change can happen, in the heart
of thinking about things. My famous feelings.

2.

Cision, a cutting. A strange word. Gonxha was Mother
Teresa's childhood name, how does it sound.
Just before she died she said "I cannot breathe."
There is an accuracy there. We must know
what we can do. Every breath is a decision.

3.

But who's deciding? The breath decides how to flow,
the horse decides where the rider goes. In the power
of our instruments, we plan a revolution. Or a vacation.
Or building a stone house to put some gods in,
on an elephant house for the local zoo. We float along
content to have been decided. Why tonight is different.

4.

Tonight there must be a decision. I feel it in the air
like football season, something to do with other people
(I hate football), some deciding about them. Here it is,
the moment is at hand, I am deciding right now.
Without even knowing the stipulations, the conditions,
without even knowing the alternatives, I choose.

5.

Long after it is made I receive the coded instruction
which I can use to understand the implications
of this decision. I know it's now and that is all I know.
But I decide it. It has to do with everyone
one by one. I turn to see what I have said.
I sleep now to find out what I have done.

RURITANIAN ELEGY

If I were a semi-suicidal poet in a small country
using a frail endangered language only natives love,
my fragmentary observations would become
a guide to life and death for all occasions
and lead countless intense young readers into hell.

How fortunate for my karma and the world
that all my propositions and discoveries
are embedded inside a formidable castle of text,
almost unreadable experiments, unbearable
revelations of the most trivial desires, heart
attacks of sheer prose. My readers uniformly
fall asleep before they ever reach my bad advice

then wake up with a start, vaguely comforted to know
that somewhere someone loves somebody, maybe
even them, silhouettes hard to make out
coming over the crest of the hill in morning fog,

sea-bell bonging, nothing clear,
and nobody's really ever figured out
how much good love does anyhow.

MANDRAGORA

If I pull up the mandrake root
the scream will drive the dog inside me mad

and away he'll run. I'm left
with a root in my fingers (but I had a root

already), a root like a man puts you to sleep,
lulls the lover in the throes of surgery,

she wakes up cured, all her dogs
have also run away; she gets up,

puts on her purple gown and walks in the grass,
stripes of opaque, stripes of sheer,

no barking to be heard, no news from anywhere,
just her bare feet and mid-morning lawn still wet,

Emerald, she thinks, with dew diamonds
there and here. Then she decides to read her hands:

this small hand also pulled a root
till it came out of earth, and once a root is taken

what is the ground to do? All this folklore, she thinks,
all these stars and names, dim protocols

of ancient vanished peoples disguised as what I feel.
What I think I feel. Why should my lovely skin

take such pleasure from the dew-eyed grass?
And whom does pleasure serve? What is my body for?

THE NOBLE SUITOR

Anything, anything.
No one to tell.

I ring my bell
and walk in shade.

No art or trade,
just marrying.

I am the noble suitor
come to touch

I turn myself
into your story,

I am the noble suitor
come to ask

does the silver mask
I wear to hide

my leprosy inside
seem somehow truer,

that unchanging smile
lives inside your dream

like a distant gleam
after all the weary miles

of forest, caves, desire?
Come kiss the simple fire

of my faithless lust.
I am a fatal glory

come to be the heart
of your story

and turn it into me,
make you my wife

and take away your life.

SUDDENLY

I want to call my mother
and see how she is
but I don't know the number of the dead

the dead, the gone, the turbulent
voices hurry through me,
I am not calling, I am only answering.

What happens to a glass when you see through it,
what happens to a hand
when there is nothing to touch?

WRITING: FOR MOSES WAS
A STAMMERER

Not being free to say,
I smote a rock
with characters. I wrote.

I was the god
of what I meant.

Writing is the exact sign of repression as well as its actual mechanism. Every child knows this. The sensory experience is lost into the word, the word is lost into its sound, then the sound is lost into the written word. Then the eye dreams the word into new interior, vivid, half-conscious life.

The stammered word sticks to the page.

Burial of affect in the memory trace.

But from it new áffect rises,

to afféct us. To make us feel. No matter who we are.

Writing is memory. Writing is remembering experiences we never had.

Writing is alien memory injected into us, so we feel again what we never felt.

In Exodus, God's finger traces the commandments on the rock — engraving the repression and the repression's law at one and the same time, in writing. He *talks* to Eve and Adam, but he *writes* to Moses's people, the chosen people, the people signed by his written will. No wonder Aaron doubts! Aaron and his kin, realists that they are, realists and lovers, are nervous always about this new law, this law that writes itself all over their experience, that talks to them *from inside themselves* — because that is where written language sounds, come to expression.

The written word speaks from inside you now. You become its only voice.

The Jews received a written law, and lost the liberty of their own interior silence. Ever after, Judaism and its children — Christianity, Islam, Liberalism — have to strive to recover the interior silence, the *sacred absence previous to the law* — but that somehow must be harmonious with the law. And isn't that the mystic's work, the meditator's?

Moses too, at the end of Schönberg's great unended, finally unspoken, opera, Moses will say "Word, Word, Word I lack" — but the German seems to blame the word: *Wort, Wort das fehlt mir* — word that fails me, word that denies itself to me, word that is missing, lacking,

the word lost
into the written text,
lost in the repression —

all the rules
through which the lover,
listening hard,

can sometimes hear
— or think to hear —
someone's actual mouth.

BRUCKNER

The style of the man is what I love,
the pope in him doming and throning.

Men like him live not in fear of rejection
but of defilement. Like losing your mittens
because you're staring at some girl.

Or leaving your knitted cap on the train
because you were distracted by beauty.

No wonder cathedrals reach into the sky —
nothing there to soil your hands with,
no beauty to break your simple heart.

Infinite space to structure
no limit to the love you pour
up and out in edge-less striving.

To come back to a place
you've never left
and see the old moon
still leaning on the ruined barn

and watch the stream
still rivering. And the trees'
stiff alphabet
still rehearsing signs

you still can't read,
a love-letter from the future
sealed with a kiss
but from whose lips?

SONATINA

Bringing something to mind is the same
as bringing it to God, the way
Mary Goodlett used to re-pot flowers,
sinister green live-forever house plants — but she
died — jade plants, dracaena, mother-in-law's tongue
— the way we walked along the ditzy little stream
at Smith in cover of darkness holding hands.

To remember well is to be close to God.
That is the saintliness of Proust,
to taste again the wasted time, and offer it,
offer it up, all time made sacred by the act —

fact — of bringing it to mind. Say it to God.
Some of her plants are still living
here and there, shivering like us
in the February wind, surviving still, naked
as Achilles among his enemies.

PUBLIC SPACES

Sometimes in the gaunt cathedral
to know a hand has reached
up out of fear and turned
loneliness into architecture —

secret of Justinian, secret
of Bach, to build out
from the absence
that is your center,

build out
a circumference
until it touches
all there is.

Everyone who comes inside
stands equally entitled
to the roof, the distance,
the geometry of God.

THE GOLDBERG VARIATIONS

Specifics are all we ever need. Intrusion from Heaven of the First Theme. It could be the first word ever hummed in the world, first music, first heard. How anything begins. How all of sin and arrogance

is emptied like the thought of suicide when pain goes away. End of theme one. Pain is driven out by pleasure. First variation. I demand a cobbler make me shoes will let me naturally saunter

deep inside the body of a woman

not just anyone

not just a beauty but the one the one

heartbeat palpitation healthy heart my blood pressure 135 over 56

this is my week Variation 2 Lust monopolizes. There is a science in these matters. Once I stood in Leipzig by your grave. The light was like today two years ago cold spring. Third variation. A Saxon song, a dance for Turkish acrobats — did you see them in Dresden, Potsdam, Magdeburg?

It is better on the piano than on the threshing floor. One does not smell the dancer's sweat though one makes love. One does barely hear their practiced smile.

Sometimes you're so Balinese! The way your fingertips bend subtly backwards, shape the air in narrative persuasions. As if I understood the least thing of what you tell me, but I stand and smile and would not for a moment turn away from such a tuneful body swayed.

And now I've made you sad, by talking such physics, and I'm sorry. Unclean matter! Yet you are all we have. And if I were in India again I would listen to you still, your long compassion.

Because you have worked your way into my collarbones and deeper still, into capillaries, wandering cells of this and that that must be me. Where the Golgi bodies encode their protein messages obedient to your rhythm. You drive me crazy.

Because you drive me. All the sensuality you evoke but never discuss, leave it in my lap as if it were mine alone!

All the sex you send. All the intellect's ardor shining like an October sky — but never a word to pollute that purest understanding. *Binah*, said the Cabbalists, the knowledge in experience, the sorrow of every thing that knows it's a composite of all other things. Experience is such a sad song, Johnny.

The light falls on our faces from afar — and that is all we know. It is here and came from there.

O Queen of Elsewhere how sleek your gown sways as it brushes over my bare knees. This music nakeds me. We're so close in this world. A meek thought can't help but touch a thousand minds. Crowded, crowded, all these hands reach out to know me.

Christ, it's like a field of flowers that I am, and you the wind.

The wind that knows me.

Flowers in the Sachsenplatz outside the church you shaped the air to hear me. Why do I know myself better in your music than outside? Thomaskirche. Blue and yellow flowers colors of Saxony I think.

You never knew the Brandenburg Gate, of course, never knew the poisoned lake of Wannsee Germany, the sick repentant Germany of self-sadistic socialism, the Stasi headquarters a block or two away from your church. The triumphalist Germany of after-me-the-deluge. You knew only the Prussian skies, and they are no different.

An old woman in the woods still speaks in the old language. Wend. You must have known more than a word or two of it, you have so much Asia. So much Asia.

Holzweg. Sometimes the path loses the way. *Irrlicht.* Sometimes the lights do not show the future but only the blue baleful corpse fire of what we are coming from. When a man follows that will o' the wisp or jack o' lantern, he is led deeper into the ago, and he is gone. Past light is the bleakest gleam, please do not let us hear that light.

And is what we need a Viking fire, a wading fast ashore, killing with wet knees and a rusting sword we have been so long at the slaughter. Hammer steel. So soon the world will rust, our northern purity corrode.

Crucible and sword, rune in stone, a hot philosophy.

Let it be after all a river.

A bow drawn, three hearts, a continent to bid. A pair of hearts. Montezuma weeping in his palace. Yes, you knew all about that, all about America, old news already in your time. George Washington was eighteen when you died.

Old news is best. We know how to mourn to its measure.

Silvery permissions. I hear an ultimatum in this music, an ultimatum with a bony back, prominent collarbone, an essay on remorse, private woe, though we all dream the same moon into the sky.

TWO SOUND NETS TO CATCH THE DARK

1.

So many be you and few a restaurant
bulldogged by common sense a father
grieving for someone else's son because an ill
opened up inside sad flourish towards form
that knows no planetary analemma,
distortion of dosa, who is waiting in the magma
under Etna under anybody I grieve
for me when I heard you grieving I heard
a lost mathematician stumbling milkweed
stalk grass through sidewalk cracks one
tall homeless loping proposition searching
margin wide enough to write the proof down
full but lord the whole world is not broad
enough to inscribe even the shortest sentence.

2.

That is the augury of the auspicious landsman
sailing a seagull caught in the museum serenity of book
at midnight with no moon to bother us so
far away the escalators and men in mango shirts
try to prove something to the ethical police
all coins are made to fit the hand imagine otherwise
stone money of the isle of Yap we used to read about
Christ a book will tell you anything you never
can tell what you are told the ragman may once
have been the muffin man the sandman is your mother
your father is weeping all the theories in the world
have come to kiss the baby in the crib and she
is weeping too because the lake is too quiet the night
is cold the dear restaurants are roaring with denial.

THE ASCENT

All you are is feeling. And a bird
stoops down from the sky
and takes your mind.

You say: I have been carried
into heaven. And there I saw
a splendor on God's chair,

a wave of murmuring consciousness
all round the throne
small leaves bursting out on spring's first tree
and I can't tell if anyone is sitting there.

I caught a bird out of heaven
and begged him to tell his name.
He said We have no names at all,
you're the ones with names.

I held him in my hand,
warmer than brown,
warmer than red, held him
to my ear to hear his word.

He had no word. I heard his heart
frolicking against the dark inside
he tries to fly away from all his life
higher and higher into blue nowhere

and again he asks What are they for,
these names you cherish and insinuate?
But I thought: I hold you to my heart
and said so, and pressed him

gently to my heartbone, and let him listen
till he cried out gently Now I understand,
now I know what you mean, a word
is what we do inside that anybody else

suddenly can hear. You have one too.
At first I thought you only were a hand.

OMENS

1.

Flowers on the locust tree
means lightning's near.

Sunlight on an empty road
means a dream you'll have tonight
and never lose.

White water splashing in a dark ravine
means Mars and Uranus combine
to make you fall in love with someone wrong
who gives you everything you need.

2.

Pay the rent means work till night.
Start the car means Plato's right.

Chop the wood means don't pretend.
Answer the phone means friendships end.

3.

Then the broken cart begins to roll
the dead man lumbers through the street

a carnival is moving into town
in front of tarnished mirrors husbands practice lies

and when the last lie has been told
I'll be young and you'll be old.

THEN ABEL FIRST SLEW ADAM

and Adam rose
saying Cain is my preference, my spear, my vegan
attitude, my fierce resistance, Cain is my maquis
against the fascist overlords of life.
And blessed him
with the Star of Exile (looks like an aleph)
and sent him off howling
into the deserts east of language
where only meanings live
empty-hearted among the tamarisks.

Meantime Abel slept, and dreamed the Bible.

It was a book to take his sin away
but daddies don't stay dead

(books stay written, this book especially,
that must be read inside out and upside down
to get the true story to shake out).

Fathers keep rising up, putting on
their cocked hats like an admiral,
their academician's sword, mason's apron,
electrician's tool belt, keep rising up
into the atmosphere of Enviable Accomplishment

so book after book has to be written down
fast to keep these ghosts away.

For phantoms flee language,
language is Eve's answer, Lilith's invention
on loan to her younger sister Eve.
For Lilith is the night, and of the rib of Night
poor Adam was made.

Therefore Night is always yearning for a man
       and a good man is most himself at night
safe in the body of his mother wife.

And all of this is Abel's dream,
dream of snow and dream of sand,
dream of woman, dream of man,
Abel, whose name is *hevel*, 'empty, vain,'
the personless name who sleeps in emptiness.

A MUSCLE IN THE MIDDLE OF THE MIND

1.

Nobody talks my language.
Are we supposed to be lovers
or are we just leaves on the same tree

far away maybe from the trunk that unions us,
so far away we don't know we are one
vegetable speeding in a common light?

And all goes Easter with the alien moon.

2.

The Minister of Atonement sleeps at her walnut desk.
The Minister of Forgiveness plans his suicide.

Rain tracked onto the marble floors of the ministry
is mopped up by old women. The Minister
of Weather kneels on the doorstep and prays to the rain.
The Minister of Departures is reading a little brown book.
On soft old paper it tells the miracles of Christian prayer
and how the opening of St John's Gospel
is like a shield to wear that keeps you safe from
dangers of body and soul — ghosts, pestilence, and war.
I used to say it all the time.

STILL LIFE: ORIGIN OF
THE ALPHABET

Between the fading fuchsia-spotted lily and
the budding iris, I am like some florist's fern
(from northern California rainwoods rustled wet)
shoved in a glass jar by brutal ikebana
to show off someone else's colors. I am no rose.

Back in the bathroom the alphabet's still ripening,
waiting for Ancient Semites to wake up and notice
hello, these birds *leave* their shadows on the ground
behind them when they fly away. Kabbalah
is the art of wondering where the birds are now.

ALARM CLOCK STUNNED BY SUDDEN DAWN

velle non discitur
—Seneca

The lady in the cartoon next door dreams of Spain
as if it were all dark hair and poetry.

Why would anybody ever want to go anywhere?
What's the matter with being here? Even the sun
comes here every day — at once an argument
in our favor and a reminder to be gone.

I am rooted in staying, like sap in maples,
lost in a universal dream of suck.

                                        Silly old
gentlefolk pursue lost youth in Oldsmobiles,
they're all like minor figures in Jane Austen

you smile at and right away forget. Forever,
usually, if space lasts that long.

                              Ah, there he is
with his ultimates again, his firefly
philosophy, a Casanova with brown paper bag
over his head, he hurries in the moveless world

he has enough going for him to get there
wherever it is, and be deemed intelligent
along the way.

                    Because intelligence
is really just wanting things a lot
and getting them. Trying to leave
stains on the walls that weren't there before.

DYNAMITE

The dust lifts,
gravel scatters,
dust falls. The animals
are beside themselves

caught in their longest
tradition: terror.

The frightened
snake's heartbeat
a dark star
I hear in my chest.

RK: *Son épitaphe*

Who is my peace?

What upright
oak or doom
shelters rare
deity? Rococo
comparisons
rainswept simple.

Druid I die
who lived caparisoned
in dozen faith.
                  Sweltering
in the winters of philosophy
I set my mark
on language
the flimsiest stone

or in closed rooms the pale
green sacrament of dust.

THE FARMER

Once there was a farmer
left his seed. He was a woman
and planted deep over horizon.

Once there was a rainstorm
and it ate her field. Once

he was covered with blood, once
the blood was language
and talked back, his fingers hurt,

his wheat walked, he heard
them coming up the hall at night
when she lay in her bed remembering
what it feels like to forget. Quiet,

dear mind. Say nothing, sea.

Earth and water, fire and air — once
was a farmer who wasn't there,
guesses made out of falling snow, a hand
suddenly slipping into your own.

WHOEVER GOES TO THE MIRROR /
NEVER COMES BACK
—Hans Jürgen von Winterfeld

Forty-three years ago a poem beginning with those lines
was published in *Botteghe Oscure.* Today I lifted the volume down,
shabby old Italian paper soft as a minor actress murdered in
      the rain,

and read those terrifying words.
I remember that time after time I and all like me
(I mean you, I can't exist without you,

can't be without that music) walked down the hallways in vanity
and stared into the all-too-bright contradiction in the glass
and that image became me and went on its way

that had been my way and is just its way now,
a logical regression into the catastrophes of optics
where all the lines of sight converge in hell.

I left myself in the glass and found you there
on your way to an identical disaster, your eyes passed through me
(because there was nothing left of me) and studied the ruin

identical with your beautiful face. Then you too turned
and all of us retreat into the company of those
who have looked once at their faces and turned away.

JOHN YAU BY CANDLELIGHT

I caught your face once
between two flames,
hell's choir boy
you looked to me,
a meditator,
a young prince of between.

As between Aix and Avignon
a ruined castle stands
much visited by swallows
who hover high
unbeatingly on a thought of air

for thought is warmth.
A thought is a face
between two candles
stuck in the dark,

a face that looks back at you
as if it knew something
nobody can possibly know.

DIRT ROADS

Who is the heart?
We have to know
the littlest things.

1.

every rock
is where once was

some pain
that once said me

2.

stall for time's
vocabulary

make a video
of common light

play it in the hollow

scooped out of night
with your wanting

the plunge of one into

3.

Aporias.

Somebody's word

come to the end
again and again

no end to the end
no before to before

every footstep
the final
every breath the last

every road a wall

4.

or reaching out in the dark
find the hollow
place below your throat

a jewel might rest there
amber amethyst
a god

5.

sparrows soar
out from underneath her skirts
rebel watchfires
flicker prairie

inside the fusebox serpent coiled

sometimes nostalgia
for an old country
never seen
a home you never had

travel the way a steeple stands

6.

geologist of the merest argument
you can't win with me
I stand under your last word
staring straight up at the moon it means

7.

someone spoke
of the flight of cranes

we live of course
by other people

their deaths their agonies

8.

who gives a breath
gives a sign

we are all too drunk
to fail to understand

9.

give waiting to music
the way you'd give
water to horses

10.

going to sleep
is like reading a Chinese dictionary

everything is new in your hands

we sleep at night
because the birds stop talking then

and waking up
the book falls out of your hands

everything has meaning
and nothing makes sense

11.

who is this light on the carpet
who wrote this silence

12.

In our century the destiny of the individual
presents itself under the symbolism of the window
peered into at night from outside, the garish spectacle
of our private lives thrown on the walls of the mind

or gazed out of in silent mornings,
a householder from the dubious security of her house
stares blankly at the enterprise of otherness
we vaguely call The World.

The night vision and the day version
are psychoanalysis and politics,
the Voyeur and the Commissar.
In both cases the window signifies

Other people are strange and probably don't love me,
are dangerous, have things I don't have, and are far.
So when we say A Person
we mean A window of one's own.

13.

Dear window
who knows
where I stand

who knows
where the light comes from
that makes me see

that makes me me?

14.

Dear Color
everything lives in you.

Kandinsky and Albers
do business here with us,
as us, the rest
is just the checks we write
drawing on the everlasting Red.

Dear Color
let me sleep and wake with you,
and dine in your arms,

Color does all our thinking for us,
Color answers all questions
with its single own,
Color asks us in all its voices
Are you me yet?

How can there be a book
colored like a bruise
like the silk she wore
in a dream only I had I thought

but you had too
whose hands stained this paper
long before the words got here
to stain the stains.

How can there be a color
nearer to me than my skin

or her skin even,
that never-ceasing violin?

15.

unclothe the other
from the veils of time
the sleazy double-knits of history

I am the elder
nuder than Susannah
no matter all my tallises

you see my naked time

16.

Belshazzar's feast in every glass
interpret the scary words
as kanji of light
caught in our eyelashes
we stare at the sun and read

the words the light tells me
I have told

17.

the mind fumbles with their names
like a drunk with his girlfriend's bra
trying to get each memory open
to feel the actual flesh of who they are

18.

I'm an air sign,
air signs don't prepare.
Instead they despair.
Generally things work out
a little better than they feared.

This modus operandi
comes in handy
when you wait for transportation
in some calamity,

or walking to the podium
with not an idea in my head —
that's the best way, see what comes up
when my back is to the wall,

that's the part of life that interests me:
to see what I'll say in such extremity.

19.

it helps me not to take too seriously
what is so mysteriously
obvious in daily use,
a fuck-up with sixty volumes of excuse

20.

ragamuffin clouds
begging some
baksheesh from the sun

21.

five swans flying
south in a line
low over river

past steel oil tanks
on the Kingston shore
ice floes, a sheet

of ice midstream
moving with the birds
I am rigid with cold

and something more
the warm thing too
that sends the swans

22.

and who told you
to be me

who let the pronouns
breed in their blessed cages of our flesh

and spawn such monstrosities of love

23.

bundle of strings
we hold together
and hold one another
to this strange
dream we call a fact

24.

The similitudes of Lord Jesus
may be likened to Dew
deposited on a desert rose.
Or a cluster of blue grapes
proffered to a dusty traveler.
A chest full of old books.

We have marched into the sky
to find our roof, tectum,
the head of our house

to weave from light
our text. All we are
is answers to a lost question.

25.

for language cannot swim
language is the ocean

waves move only up and down
the movement we call meaning
stirs along the swell

never gets there never gets lost

26.

The parachute.
Ménage à un,
this love affair
falls down the air.

Everyone
is going to die
except I.
I was never born,

is nowhere
to be found,
just hangs around.
Were you ever

a brick wall,
mermaid, library,
postcard of the full moon
sent home

as if you'd been there
and there is some here
to which the mail
can come,

this is winter
that Irish music,
and ice is a diamond
of impediment,

a Roman word that means valises
the airline loses
full of underwear and socks and manuscripts
purporting to be by me.

27.

makes no sense to keep a diary
since all I am is telling

and no seabird does
mournful creature Whitman celebrates
some lonesome gannet falling through a porphyry
cloud like a fleshy smile, a lonely bird
whose mate made not this rendezvous alas
o god the solemn absences of space
with winter crashing on the empty shore

28.

and churches think they need an organ —
just open the fucking window and the wind will
weep all the Jesuses you'll need
truth upon truth till the year is green again

never, and Armand doesn't die, and Mary didn't,
or Paul, Charles, Robert, Marcia, April,
Joel, Louis, Jack, Steve, Amy, Allen, Ruth
or my root Lama or my father or my mother

or anybody's anybody, and in one
of Fomenko's columns of brainless statistics
thank God Adam too is still alive, all the numbers
happen all at once, the organ plays,

nobody dies, 'nothing happens,' we call it music,
it is time rushing past the shabby porches of our ears

and I am just a terrible mistake

    29.

You never have a clue to who you are
until you feel your back against the wall
and there is nowhere to go but who you are.

    30.

the dome and its minarets float above the sea

everything is a reflection of their desires
who persuaded it to be
don't you know the skin knows everything?

THE VIEW FROM MICHIGAN AVENUE

Blake's *Urizen* — rocks above him, contoured to fit him? — or is he breaking his body's way out of the encompassing material? Is there a difference between these two questions? What is striking is that the rock above him — pale, distempered, flecked with umber — is blotched and patterned with shapes that instantly remind me of Lascaux: bison, leaping beasts.

Guardi's *capricci* — imaginary landscapes. One capriccio is shown: ruined arch or vault. What better gift can an artist render than an imaginary landscape? Especially one that's right here. This is even better to sail through than his Venetian canalscapes.

John Makepeace's chair. Dorset, now. All willow pale and yellow. A beautiful thing. It's not like anything else, and not very different either. It stopped me in my tracks at the foot of the steps. It stays with me now, a chair like a cool idea.

Bourdelle's *Héracles the Archer*. After all these years I finally see it in the bronze — how long I studied it in the plates that illustrated the article on Sculpture in the old *Britannica*. It is small. It sits on a table. He draws his bow against the Stymphalian birds, I take it, who are nowhere nearby. They heard me coming, they heard his bow creaking as he bent it, and have flown away over the immense lake.

The Portland Vase. Wedgwood. Designed by Henry Webber. How many copies of this are in the world? Which is *The* Portland Vase? I remember Wolf Mankowitz's *My Old Man's a Dustman* and the boy's fixation on the vase, touchstone of all culture, beauty, escape.

We should mightily enlarge Blake's color work, the tinted and painted-on monotypes, his quiet splashes — examine them under magnification, and what would we find? The Lascaux resemblances in the *Urizen* (the *Book of Urizen* vintage) — amazing prefiguring of

85

an art that would not rise into awareness for another hundred years, when the caves gave up their living.

If we enlarged these Blakes, what languages would we see? His bent for language, logos, story, may have guided him, the way he dreamed with his hands. And silent Catherine, his wife, steeped in both their dreamings, she too may have cast her dream into smudge and stipple. All we have to do is read. Every mark is language. Every mark contains a microscopic text we bend to read. That is what the old rabbis meant by Looking down to find God. We must bend deep, reverent, over every mark and destroy its calm indifference into a meaning we read. A meaning we need to read. That will come to us from nowhere else in the world but right here.

Look close, arbiter of now.

Bend forward to the proffered drawing, some old master, Fragonard or de la Tour, and here you are, tiny, tiny, tiny:

your own face looks out at you
from all those busy fussy Fontainebleau leaves —

and then peer inside your microscopic eyes
and see another paradise down in there
and you, always you,
looking out.
            We cannot flee
from what we see, and who we are in seeing.

Bare trees in the courtyard of the museum: people who stood and looked and watched too long. A tree stuck in the posture of seeing, being seen.

Built on absence. The railroad runs right through this museum. Right through the nineteenth century to whatever our people call our times, post-imperial America. To get from one building to another go down to the bottom floor. Railroad through it. Built on absence. We still have our push, our hunger for the material embodiment of what we thought. The fetish. A road runs through our staying. Us, our, we, ours — no meaning to this apparently yummy plurality. I am a majority.

Therefore I built my house in a lake, like the ancestors, and built of stone like my grandsires, a house on stilts, a house on bedrock, half wood half stone, I live in it now, and who are we in all this me-ing?

A seagull has a blissful cast of wing, bluish in some lights, some lakes, we see her pass between us and the light.

Spurs of witness goad our dull nag, this sleepy hour in the sculpture court while God's own weather wastes its time above our head.

For art means war. We battle against the commonest relax.

Who knows who may strive with us, popes and procurers and princesses — authority is an apple every kid finally has to learn how to steal.

Sometimes I want to turn away from everyone.

Tintoretto's Lucretia: as Tarquin grabs her from behind, her pearl necklace breaks — the pearls are falling as we watch, falling like the lights in the Tree of Life down her body: two at the heart, one at the navel, one at the pubis, one at the vulva, one at the knee, six rolling out below her feet.

In Titian's Danæ, the jeweled bracelet on her right wrist mirrors or rhymes with the jeweled collar on the little lap dog asleep just beneath her hand. As the collar is the sign of the dog's enslaved condition, so is the bracelet of hers — enslaved by her desire for jewels, gold, power. Jupiter is an old man hurrying down to take advantage of her appetites.

Orbiting in passion
among the silver
cylinders of Arthur Dove,
world's strangest

painter. Marsden
Hartley's *dead*
sea dove in the same
gallery, these

beautiful Americans.

Of course from memory.
Bourdelle's Hercules.
Balzac courtesy
of Rodin. All smaller
than you'd think

as if a hero is a puny thing
the mind makes big
going over and over
a few significant deeds.

Caillebotte on the street, Guardi
on the piazza, Hubert Robert
painting almost life-sized
the impossible temples of the mind.

No Vermeer's view of Delft.

No wonderful Dutch synecdoche — a woman, a window, a brick, a scrap of lace — and all the miles and money of the world come easy to our calm loving mind. All the commodity and relationship of society made plain by this or that well-chosen scrap of evidence. This is so unlike the pitiless detail of Italianate allegory, where everything the reader needs to understand is glossed pictorially inside the frame, and a picture seems to be composed of a visual index of the icons of its meaning. Dutch synecdochical austerity depends utterly on the viewer's savoir faire — which is probably why Charles Swann, flattered, was so fond of Vermeer.

And Zurbarán's Crucifixion is exactly what I had in mind when I wrote about a crucifixion in hyperspace. Yidam figure isolate on empty ground. There are no mourners, mothers, Marys, thieves. Just God dying in the black sky.

Giovanni di Paolo's six panels of the life and death of St John the Baptist. The going off into the hills (we see him setting out, the road is big, we see him far away, just the same but smaller) is a perfect image of the Buddhist home-leaving, the Milarepa gesture. The beheading itself, the saint's neck hangs down from a window like a goose neck cut. The wheedling Salome all slim and blonde and well-kept hair.

Headless seated Buddha in stone, from Indonesia. Life-size. What is the size of a Buddha's life. It strikes me as very beautiful, like the other images from Indonesia, with an intensity, an ardor, a working power greater than that of images from the Buddhist heartland. Is the art of a religion fiercer, more expressive, more effective out at the missionary fringe? Indonesia, Japan, Tibet rather than northern India. Just as Christian art finds its culmination not in Palestine or even Rome, but in Holland, Russia, France.

89

Gossamer, memory is gossamer. It's fading, drying out like dew on a cobweb, drying as I speak or write down what I fancy I remember. Speaking is *dismembering*. Silence recollects. The act is all.

Fleshy lips of a young Pontormo, saying nothing.

MAN ON CROSS

1.

Relational aggregates
pivot
nailed to word
         engineered transference of affect
anguish needing
the pile of your carpet
         close as plush to each other

insert oboe solo here.

      Because all sense
      they make
      comes by listening.

A God dies on the hill

and such is all our music, this heap
of analytic hopes,
         dim vestments
    of an outmoded sire,
we are the children of no one
and come from heaven

         — but look at the pain
    of going back,
         Iron Nails Ran In,

there is no answer like leaving the room.

Sequences of mute ascension,

leave a lip below
　　　just wet enough to put a tongue of fire out.

We are silenced
into sanity
we who once were poetry and stuff,

once were maidens in star meadows smug.

A God is dying. The crucifixion has begun —
half an hour into it now, still
some muscular resilience in his arms,
his chest,

　　　　　　"the *something more* must be
differentiated . . .
　　　　　　　　two kinds of memory"

why did they kill my God
and why did I die on your shabby hill,

bald as an old man, bald as a horn,
as a bone,

　　　　　　two kinds of I, two
　　　　kinds of you and why
did I and why did you,
　　　　　　　a death
　　　　　　is easy to analyze,

desire's hard,
       implicit relational knowing
             of what is gone.
You came to me
a wolf around my fire

mostly I understood your eyes
golden chances

of what goes on living
why did you give

birth to me on the hill
why are you fire

why did you carve me out of bone
out of your own bone
           a little ivory man
you warmed inside your linen
between your breasts
warmed me
till I grew brown and old and big
and came out talking,

carved me with big lips big hands
a hollow where my heart is

to accommodate your bone.
Why did you give us faces?

For you are ivory too. And who carved you?

The minutes of his suffering
bend time

93

all the terrible déjà-vus of desire
fold upon fold
                    stripped from him, he remembers
every one, then none of them,

his time is bent
around us,

         not because he's deity
      but because a man
has no clock but what his body feels,

and this pain has an interesting infinity,
always welling up out of the center of him,

starfish, star-man, spread out on the sky,
beached on the hard dry sand of light,

the dry country,
               April Emperor
                          still not dead
after his three hours,
               just pain interleaved with melody,
all the memory any dying sees.

               But the Gnostics sang
      he was not what you see,
      or only what you see
                    was on the cross, and he
danced elsewhere and otherwise, or right there
dancing *lancers* round the footstep of the Tree,
he roving round and all his
dazed apostles danced with him,
                    wise fools, apprentice
knowers.

94

It is not that he did not suffer,
it is that no one does,

all of it's illusion,
        pain and dance and saying so,
illusion all,
            the mutative primacy of interpretation
is how you hold your finger to the candle flame.

There is no dying but why did they kill?
There is no pain and why do you cry,
no anguish and he groans, no music and he dances,
no God, no heaven and he walks into the sky

on broken feet, you see
the blue sky through his holes,

no feeling and nothing but feelings

they force their spirit into some kind of 'action'
                                    . . . a silence

Eye blinks of coming against each other,
or never blink your eyes,

hold fixed in seeing, all
about seeing and nothing seen,

        no object in that subject,
rapture,
all seeing and nothing seen,

he dies and there is no leaving,
hurts and there is no answer,

95

we are meeting in the mouth of parting,
a word broken to let the silence out.

2.

when they sweep the light
together over the threshold

when the light is at home in the house
and the cautious landlord snuffs his candles out

the potent husband rises in his bed
a cat puts her paw into the neglected soup
and cars roar past like circuses

it is Saturday and nothing to do
but die if you're a bull

or kill if you're a fisherman
and there will be no death

                        percussion section
        Max Roach against the gates of hell
which in those days stood in Canada

riff against dying.
When the announcer comes back on his voice
is swaddled in room noise, wrong mike
for this occasion, we want a dead,
anechoic space
                    from which the announcer
can accuse, fiddling with his bowtie,
strange how everything squeezes you round the neck,

announce
        He is risen he is not here.

But he is not risen.
Or not yet. There is a darkness in the day,
the feel of someone coming.

In patches of sunlight sit and take snuff
pondering the awesome beauty
of the last cute kids who sauntered by
walking wavy or cradling their earth-heavy plums,

anybody you can't touch is beautiful
when you are old he meant

but what he said was *She*
is the most beautiful girl I ever saw —

though the day before he'd said the same about Cézanne,
one of those sly faces the painter
hid among the apricots,

every death is about your father dying.

I know Steve Jonas
detested Charlie Parker,
had no taste for bebop
bop had no paideuma,
was the death of jazz
on Saturday at Massey Hall
among the aliens,

Steve how wrong you are I am
how wrong I am to fault you

for he is living
past the other doorway of the tomb
where he makes common cause
with Orpheus and Ashtoreth
and all the lucid deities of desire
come back with him,

        come back to me, I swear it
to you, come back to wake the world.

For Osiris is a black God
and you will never find him
if you look up there,
only down where
the voice of Orpheus is earth
giving us voice,
        standing under the song
    the riff of life
        only there
    in the dirt
  where poetry is heard

where else could I ever come from,
Delta and despair, her hair
cut off and left as forfeit
    in the dark republic

and then tomorrow Easter early
they'll come to roll away the stone
and gawk at vacancy

they'll never know they touched him promptly,
    he is the stone they rolled away,

I am the stone
    the finder's hand rejected
but I set me in the northern crown

utterly black Egypt you call the sky.

Listen to the night
say the same improving text
the ground beneath you says,

you are risen
    full of grief and language
I love it how you tread on me.

'Tulipa humilis'
    I saw its label, fuchsia-colored
            first risen small
tulip no way 'humble'
    a gaud of summer in bare-ass spring mud

and sulfury narcissus, small,

these two, beyond the crocuses, periwinkle, ground ivy —
smell of vanilla in the air
    vaginilla, little sheath,
in town the baker knelt before her lilies
'praying to the flowers?' just
'they are so beautiful'
                        I found them
    a little showy,
all rabbity for holiday,
Triduum, they say, the sacred
Three-Day
        Good Friday to Easter Sunday

but I say there's a Fourth Day
a fourth inside the three,

                        a day from Hell
when all the Harrowing is done

and Hell lets her quiet mercenaries loose
to walk our empty streets — phantom lovers,
                shadows, sweet old men
who do not lust for
                     even the fairest personages
        of our afternoon.

The Fourth Day is afternoon — Christ is down there
waking Moses up and all of them, turning
the lights on in Nirvana so they know
it's time to come to earth again and help
the weary remnant of the faithful,
                   that's all of us,
we are the chosen

and in us they speak and satirize and pour out
the luminous compassion to which we're prone,

our destiny is light
and purest jazz,
the fourth day is the god in us, ancestor,
the germ of sense

comes between Saturday noon and Sunday dawn
when Christ impersonates a stone, a gardener,
      a patient angel, a woman's
husband, a shiny phantom, a dimwit
      traveler on the road with men, a lord,
a bleeding wound, a man.

But not today.
       Today is wind
     from hell, sweet-scented

her hands full of lilacs
     in bloom down there
but not yet here
     beside bewildering rivers.

   3.

It is a relief to be risen
to lie in pale sunlight
hard, and all my veins seem now the veins of it
and all my meaning becomes its simple weight.

When a man dies, he dies into the world,
becomes it for a while until it's time
for him to sleep again, he's born
and guesses he is separate from things.

He never is, or always was, nothing
is different as difference. A man is a sister
of all things, frail where they are sturdy,
quick where they are slow. So slow.

I have to die a thousand times to be one stone.

MORPHOPHONEMICS OF
THE BLUE FLOWER

in memory of Jack Spicer

Cast one thing before another
to find out which is swine,
which is pearl.
                    You can't tell
without the casting, the couch
you wake up on, chosen
and defiled,
        or still pure
hence rejected.
You don't know which

and that is what you are,
the pronoun that knows nothing
of what I know. And I
know even less.

                We stagger
towards each other like words
in an unknown language
printed in a scruffy book you
pick up on the subway.

Are we even in the same
sentence? What is the boundary
between one word and another?
And who is silence?

SOAP

I still smell soap on my fingers.
Botticelli made me.
Made me face the naked woman
with arrogant surprise,

a little afraid. Truth is such
a sleeping dog. We are better off
with paintings on the wall.

As in Vienna where I could hardly tell
the painted faces from the women
in the museum watching them,
a voluptuous sisterhood of signs.

CHILDREN ON SUNDAY

Biedermeier afternoons in Long Island
bungalows — that's what I had in mind,
Uncle Owen with a snifter in sunshine,
his size 13½ Egyptian pima cotton
open on his scraggly turkeywattle neck.
People we love come in all sizes.

That's the sort of thing we like to talk about
while apocalyptic splendor waits
behind some trees, masquerading as
sunset on Jamaica Bay. But we know
better, we are the angels' real-estate agents —
every house door is heaven's consulate.
We know we came here for the nucleus,
the divine matinee behind the ordinary.

Movies told us first, or maybe Proust
seeing theater audience as madrepore:
colony of coral or living polyps, life stilled
for an hour to regard itself. All we are
is witnesses. I mean we're here
for the weather. To be purgatoried,
finally to wake up before the sun of our senses
is lost in the lake of day after day after day.

Sitting crazed in the kiddy section all afternoon
through serials and *Saboteur*, *The Red Shoes*,
Charlie Chan, we learned there absolutely is
no difference between movie and newsreel,
we know we are here to be beholders
of an immense transformation of which we are
simultaneously mad scientist and victim,
plus Sam Jaffe as the old Lama in Shangri-La.

IMPREGNATION OF A STANZA FROM HART CRANE'S *VOYAGES*

Mark the somber alphabet on the girl's wrist, here at the midnight
show her eyes beg for a new song turning her shoulders to
the blue wind that scours the hours
And hastens to invade her clothes, she shivers while her penniless
dawn staggers towards her rich only with sand and shabby
palms,
Pass your hands along her thin arm, let your fingertips read the
superscription all her suicides have left, scars of bent desire,
passions of seafoam and wave —
Hasten to marry her before you wake up, while all her insanities
acknowledge how truly they are true — your sleep, her death,
your shared desire,
Close your arms around one instant of her never-ending terror in
one floating cynical flower.

VARIATIONS ON TWO LINES BY ZAGHLOUL MORSY

And they say this insanity of grass is a sign of spring!
What must winter have been like if it thought all this up,
scheme upon scheme, hawk over peony, sun on my back
like an old high-school friend trying to borrow money

and the wind full of gods sweet on me from rivers.
There are so many streets I have to wear, so many
shirts I have to take off, put on, take off, never far
from that hair-trigger mirror your understanding eyes.

Of course I know who I am, *caught in a trap
of perishable signs*, I shuffle the bones
about with my paws, no, I fold you in my arms
you too have taken your shirts off, every one,

you sing to me in a logic that rises up the spine
and explains me suddenly as if it were something
I'm thinking. But by now we are past all thinking.

106

Imagine there are just as many cowboys as there are cows
and every book has its reader, like what's his name in
Wilkie Collins with *Robinson Crusoe*. And every Jew
has her Messiah, every Catholic a Vatican of his own.

Things are for us, even those most elegant of all things,
Other People. (Mes dieux, mes cieux.) And every angel
has a race apart to nurture and to supervise. Rigiel,
angel of footsteps. Ainauriel, angel of blue-eyed men.
Delethiel, angel of intruders. I mean to tell you there's no slack

and that's the grandeur and the trouble with the world,
it all comes back, can't be counted on to stay or go away.
I'd tell you more except my mind is full of peonies whose smell
lasts me all the weary daylight till you come.

ORPHEUS

the Bacchantes who tear him apart are all the women of his life —
or just the memory of them — his teachers, teasers, tellers — their
voices inside him telling him this or that — their hands inside him
pulling this way and that — their hands deep in him

because all he ever knew was to *woo* — *werben*: to be a suitor, to
woo, to compete for — and all his language was to woo them, wow
them — woo all of them and there are too many and they resent
him — they remember and they resent him — he remembers and
takes joy in their names and images and stories — then the joy
turns back on him and becomes their hands pulling him apart

how could women tear a man apart unless they had their hands
deep in him — in him and at him their resentment turns — grows
wild — they are wild — he spoke all his force to woo them — spoke
all his force to touch them — become them, even — he embodies
their bodies and they tear him apart.

VIENNA, AT THE PRATERSTERN

Blind men are walking up and down the street
singing stuff from operas, hitting the pavement with white canes

cars are stuttering under the traffic lights
the admiral is getting tired of standing on his victory column so
      far from the sea

underneath the city pale fish are swimming in the sewers
cats snake along through cellars with no desire to kill anything,
      they never have,
a man's hands are cups around a woman's
breasts he smells her hair
her face is half turned towards him she must be able to smell his
      breath

the smell of her hair he thinks
then he wonders what his breath smells like
he likes the smell of her mouth
he wonders if we all smell like the words we say

and I can't understand what they're saying,
a kind of milk you taste when you close your eyes.

THE GREAT TRAIN ROBBERY

'November day' always bracketed
we archive we weather everything
ever happened is available within
the biorama of an instant you include
yourself in the image of event

turbulent Edison documentary asides
framed as everlasting evidence the train
of associations pulls into the station
arctic birds collapse their wings against
I will give you anything to stay with me

you rainy day you encyclopedia
near friend of all the distances a seed
is not more compact than this flame
upright on the citronella candle shielded
from the little light the little wind I breathe

when you breathe people in you know
the taste of what they're feeling never think
always meditate the truth is lighter
than anybody thinks the lies a sediment

settles out of solution as the bandits
swarm over the halted express their guns
smoke silently sound has not been invented
death is a silent pirouette and wheat
sprouts quick along the broken track.

THEORY OF THE WORKING CLASS

1.

Why is Marx's gospel always beginning
Liebestraum in the open air
why can't I speak English the stones my
fathers did, contented themselves with rustic
music, Greenpoint eloquence, cattlecar
philosophy. We are enslaved by
what makes us free — intolerable
paradox at the heart of speech.

2.

All labor belongs to me because I perceive.
One by one its benefits a crystal rosary
of intimate occasions and worlds new made
a bead for each one you touch o mow
the lawn love and rebuke this green theosophy.
Labor is the value that we add to fact
brute suchnesses of grain and ore
the farmer is invented by his seeds.

TURF FIRE

I come to you as weather after all

the distances I thought were mine
walk around in the dark. Dark children
sing skeptically in little languages.

No one knew me, and no fault but mine.
I was hidden from the beginning
and when I tried to show myself I used your face.

AN EPISODE OF PARISH HISTORY

Understanding the analysis of space
he built a mountain. Having read
two or three books about light
he built the sun.
                        When the new
universe was ready he moved in.

The neighbors called it suicide,
the priest said some prayers
over the old sweater he left behind,
and sprinkled holy water on the footprints
that led from the back door and stopped
suddenly three yards beyond the rowan tree.

Falcarragh

SNAIL

A gatherer
of distances
          I swallow miles
the way a snail I had
in Flatbush once
swallowed the thread of a lace
curtain, ate his way to the top
of the cloth — then where was he,

him with all his distances,
with all his outsides inside?

He had reached the top of the window
and run out of light.

Dublin

THE CRANES OF MESTRE

in memory of Paul Blackburn

Sky-fast over the scribbled
passenger trains, the walls
blue and magenta with graffiti.
Earth is the place where people write.

Words on walls, henna palm-prints of Moroccan Jewesses
placed firmly, sweaty against white plaster

that's what I see when I look out the train window
into the place outside I call my heart
as if a bird could fly from the hand to the wall.

The sky itself had a message in it once
that years of looking long ago rubbed out.

THE LITTLE TESTAMENT

Bellflower beyond repair
autumn everywhere

and I for once congratulate
the human season

the sun has bothered me so long
the little political rain

seems to cheer the rhododendrons
who were they in a former life

strippers in the Tenderloin
I forgive your clothing

as I have done so often
tossed it into the dark

this pale millennium
between the red disclosures

I want a naked galaxy
my poor soul

electric blue carrying
this oafish reticule of flesh.

THE EAR OF ORPHEUS

When cells multiply the world divides.
Or did he mean it the other way round
when he spoke on the wrong side of my ear —
                                    always
                    we talk about Orpheus singing
but what could it be if Orpheus *hears*

you can never tell with angels,
                who are all telling anyhow.
I stand corrected, like a bishop of the obvious.
Listen to me, his honor said, when cells
do it fiercely in the night, splitting and spitting
                like cobras, the world unifies
into speculums — victim mirrors —
                to gaze up inside galaxies,

that morbid curiosity we call Light
penetrates the meekest mysteries.
Equals, we are equals, a man and I,
                an angel and its listener rapt
in the acoustic fuck, the blue
amplexus of the ear.

            Deep ear. Listen to me, his grace went on,
I give you fellowships and chronic ailments,
give you sunlight and glaucoma, give you oatmeal,
everything, I am your life,
                    won't you listen?

But Orpheus will not listen to his life.

His life is dead and three times now
he has crept down the cellar stairs to hell,
that long blue movie, and the unreal police
set their dogs on him. Real poets hate dogs,
didn't you know that?
                    His life is dead
and three times he went down the creaking stairs
to fetch her back
                    from her abstraction there.
Whitewash and laundry tub and coal,
                              the devil very small
          a kind of nimble centipede red-plumed between bricks

and the devil told him: you can have her back
          if you can make her listen
                    (I can't, she is all hearing
and no listening)
          and then if you can make
                    yourself listen to her
(you are all hearing)

                              and from where she lingered
          measuring the fall of dust through light,
all the dust of the world
          that gives things their shapes and colors, falling,
she heard her husband
          since she was all hearing, and moved with him
three times up the crumbling staircase
          to the castle parapet to watch the Turkish stars
unfurl over ocean,
                    she never left him
(I never left you)

she died into him (I die into you)
her life is in him now (I live in you)

and he doesn't know it. I know it, only sometimes
when I hear my own voice
            it sounds like her
                            (it sounds like you)
he thinks it's her (I know it's you)

my life, my life,
            all cells and listening
to make you speak (you make me speak)

and finally there's no telling what the other angel said.

THE LETTER

I was trying to write you a letter,
        a letter like shiny beads
                of that grease-lustered jet
the Romans liked so much, they got it from Whitby
        up the Yorkshire coast where natives
still set it out for sale
        in little shops on little streets
under the red tile roofs and a cold fog,
be there with me,

                                        a black

        almost angry semi-precious
                (what a strange value) stone.

It looks angry. I wanted to write you an emerald
        to take anger away,
                dissolve it in the sea of pure looking,
look at it, look in it, look through it, wanted
to write you an ocean
                to wash away anger,

wanted to write you an incense letter
        to light a stick from an angry candle
then blow the candle out,
                                I was trying
to write you a letter like a geode
        hard to crack and beautiful at least.

I wanted to write you a letter made of oil
        would come off on your fingers and stain your clothes
                with sleek translucency
so you'd look down and say yes that's him,
        that word at least is authentic, it almost hurts.

I was trying to write you a letter on lace,
        to be beautiful, symmetrical and see light through,
a letter like beeswax, chewy, sweet, read it in its own light,
        it's so hard to read the light itself,

                        wanted
            to write you a letter like sugar,
easy, melting, it makes you fat, your flesh
        remembers me for you,
                was trying
to write you a letter like birds
        flocking intricate down the sky at evening
over the river,
        our energies isomorphic, all parallels, we fly
when we are really who we are,
        not birds, not stewardesses, not angels,
not insects or butterflies or bats,
we fly winged with each other

                        sick with separation
        we fly together, all the molecules
                align in the vessel,
                                three years
and not finished, never finished.
                        I was trying
to write you a letter made of glass
        you read it by smashing it on the windowsill
then all day long the sun reads the words of it back to you
glare by glare, and sometimes drowns them out
        shouting the blue of light

as if the whole business of the world was
        writing a letter to you too.

EXPERIENCE

A river is a cloud nobody remembers.

So when the steeplejack falls from the bridge tower
almost effortlessly he survives,
                              he goes down
and interviews some bones
but they have nothing to tell him.
                              Everybody
is dead in the same way. Only the living
are different sometimes, for a minute or two
at a time.
                    Saved again, he sits in the café.
He has had an experience
to discuss,
                    an armature wound around emptiness.

MANOEUVRES

As by armament the soft of war
billowing round the Paris curtains

little balcony with view of square
into which the meek troupe parades

               tasting, or is it testing,
the apple-quincey acid of the air
that makes their faces scarlet
though their march is brisk,

              attend to me
the lover tugs
       hushing her back from the long window
look at me
           not those orderly vagabonds the government
exercises at our expense
       against the likelihood
of a more than Wagnerian
          love,

more than a millennial revelation,
                 come back into the room
      and be the world to me.

Round and round. Eros
      never wearies
of what he does so well,
           a will to want, and a want to fill,
and the hill goes up the Buttes Chaumont

artificial heaven as a city afterthought,

as the fountain rides the middle of the square
like a great foaming ship going nowhere,

round and round.

She turns away from watching soldierboys and puppydogs
the usual stupid fauna of the town.
But does this one look much better?
He hopes so, holding out a glass to her
steaming, tisane is it, or hot toddy,
to make her keen or make her fuzzy,
what is it we do to each other?

Is this what you want of me, she asks,
my back to the world and my face
in shadow holding you in the dim room,

only you —
is this what you want,
in the dimness of who we are
grow old till we forget the differences?

And she turns back to the square,
empty now, the pretty men
in their silly silver hats are gone,

and Don't worry, don't worry,
she says softly, maybe even whispering to him.

THE SECRET ORATOR

I passed Auden walking
fast up Greenwich one cold night
his face an agony
of inadvertent age

his young mind knew all
those wrinkles of as adages,
Novalis transports
into the blue shade of summers

yet to come and here we are
a rose at Christmas
lost in the northern world
among newborn absolutes.

1.

Inferences bid us speak.
There is a rabbi
in every cockpit
whose cantilena

prays the plane
straight as wingstruts prop
the flimsy structure
to abide the air

So ocean is sky.
Europe is a cloud we come from
over and over.
America is down there.

2.

Go down to me
companionable moon
I am your landing strip
bring me your vehicles
and highway me with light.

Arrive, twisted imperatives
of tourists, shadows
of leaves fall on the summer river,
Isar, every evening's autumn,
the stream divides,

The city around the river
is an afterthought,
a phony memory
of where I thought I was
before you came.

3.

You're the only one worth telling,
worth saying what is so or how
things come and go and fail
to make sense or just barely do.

Barely. You are manifold
a line of yet to be deciphered
hiero(=holy)glyphs along your spine
leading down to where the actual begins.

4.

And Aquinas said Marriage
is a sacrament conferred
by each upon the other,

the operators of it are the
objects of it as well, the Church
stands by and witnesses

and this witness is a blessing
but the meat of the sacrament
is your meat, man, and your

meat, woman, mingled
in the very will to mingle them
and you are married

by the fact of you
and there was no altar
but themselves.

5.

All stores sell drugs,
commodity is panacea —
across the steppe of mid-America, puszta,
the intolerable green.

There is a drug
called travel
that cures the terrible disease of being,
which always has to be somewhere.

6.

Velvet shorthairs of the nape
behind our busy thinking.

                        By proportion
            I belong to you
                    and you to me
                            by strict geometry

the fit of local propositions
                    into the universal grid.

7.

Between Sixth and Seventh Avenue
there is a tree
                    dinky enough, leaf spill mostly now, yellow brown,
ginkgo I guess,
                    a tree
to heal alertness
— but then the tree was bare —
I had to pass — him stepping down from the curb
        me stepping up — the great poet I so much loved,
I would stand before his house on Cornelia and think.

8.

There is a tree
that heals the memory too,

so that we forget
our lines

just when the audience
of all those beautiful faces,

those veiled but so palpably present beautiful bodies
squirm politely, invitely, in their destined seats.

And we who speak to them
are left without any word
previous to this moment,

left to say the new word,
the word the Masons knew,
lost, lost into now

the only where to find it is to speak.

GREEN

A blind man would be hard put to think
green, harder than any other color to imagine,

green of fire, green of tree,
green of peacock, green of mamba,

and the blind man walks among them and knows
something but I think what he knows isn't green

but how do I know what he knows but I think
nobody really knows green though I see green.

In a former life I was blind but now I see,
now I know green but maybe in a former life

there were colors and conditions I can't see now
or nobody can see, colors and textures beyond

anything I can imagine let alone name, antics
of light and wind greener than green

on the other side of the air.

THE SOUND OF THE CENTER

masaniyeh
      the tree of
death, the fatal
blossoms of opera, the plaintive
doo-wop of our ceremonies
of love

          orgasm you great tree
grows up through the core
the animal
howls at the limit of what we mean
the other speaks

that is the real sound
soft howl
wolf growl
of love coming
to love

limping through the
jungle of what you left of me
try to find a name
I can identify,
something like west or wolf
or wheat
      but all I can find
is thing after thing,
useless to me
not knowing the operative
word

so wake up
is treefall
bough breaks
baby fall
into speech

every language
is another language
when you're asleep

and no word means a thing

That's why Blake
drew so many
snakes and vines and tendrils round
the empty places where the words would be,
between the words that could be said.

The words that could be written down
are not the words,

the space between
says everything

he filled with snakes and roots and vineleaves to remind.

TWO MEDITATIONS ON THE POPE

1.

He wore an apron made of cauliflowers
strung with tough grape leaves on their vines
because he was the pope again and time
turned to the left and there he was
with a beehive on his head and the Whore
of Babylon on easy terms, he loved her
so hard he used to become her, because her style
was redder than anybody and nothing slept.
But enough of me. This pope he was
was Innocent the Lust, a gleam of plaster
on the bald spot in his rufous hair
made him glow in the dark, yes, loved to stalk
up and down the Lateran at midnight
snuffing out sputtering votive candles
here and there. *A lume spento*, like the man
said, funeral of a suicide. But life
is the cleverest suicide, thought he, and lived
a thousand years and still is living
and none of that Gershwin crap about
no gal will give in, because he still is wild
preposterous and much sought after
by the elect of either sex to know their minds.
Their beds a little after. Balls of wax
and spoons of honey, slotted spoons
to skim dead dormice from the font
where no one comes to be baptized,
why should they, life ends with life
and death's a socialism of another
stripe, wound after wound, until
we join the affably nonexistent.

2.

He would go to the movies, and lo!
there were images everywhere,
wildcat strobework flushing frescoes
green. The wall painting from some cloister
had been peeled off chip by chip
and glued to his wall, each chip
a number, each number a name of God.
Because God has to come
somewhere into this story,
it is a winter's dream, this pope in white
vegetation (mushrooms, mistletoe,
those sinister colorless
bracts of the poinsettias), this pope
who dreams in his turn corkscrew steeples,
underearth basilicas, a room one yard square
and two miles high, a room
that hangs down from a star and he
stands in the middle of it, Christ,
it all is middle, there he stands
and bleeds his hungry thinking *on the city
and the world.* And he begins
to understand his name. "We
are things to eat, that's all. And I
have done at last with eating."

THE CUP

Aparta de mí este Cáliz
—Vallejo

away from me this glass
breaks on the rock
my head rests on

traffic jam of blood and broken glass
fine angelic splinters that
pierce and sidle up the vein
my father told me
would in its own time

the time of things

the time of glass

would come to my heart and pierce
whatever it found there

a dreary meat awash in dreams

my father
take this chalice
from me
I made for myself
and filled
with everybody's wine

I wanted to get drunk on all their personhood,
the way they animate their flesh,
I wanted to know them in the instant
their minds or souls (father, what is the name
for it, the thing that makes us do,

the thing that makes us be)
I wanted to know them in the instant
when who they were poured up fast and thick and rich
into the flesh of them and what they did

I wanted to get drunk on their bodies those chalices
drunk on their souls

soil
earth
wine
wise
lost

take this glass away from me I broke on stone
take away the glass I swallowed the wine
that swallowed me

who am I talking to
what is the name I call father
what does it call itself when it's alone with the sky

does it have a glass it needs me to take away

father
I take this glass from your hands from your pain
I drink it for you at last
I drink the knowledge of men and women
always together and never together

I drink the touch of them and the letting go
I drink the drunkenness of knowing them
and the ecstatic drunkenness of knowing them in knowing you

who are the only thing around to be known

take this glass away and make it whole
like a stupid movie where the broken thing
goes backwards into its wholeness its thingness its little
piece of truth it means to be

take these fragments and make them whole
and give it back to me and let me drink

to see who I will be
because I also am a wanderer
I am not the only one with some fixed identity
I am just as vagrant as you are,
girl, hawk, wolf, god, messenger, merchant,
I am not the same as this stone I smash
glass after glass on
waiting for the hollywood miracle again and again
to bring me back together

your only river is to listen to me

take this glass and drink it full
and give it back
wild with your emptiness, father,
your personal luminous void
that I breathe in

now
after all the storms and decades of my thirst
you give me wine

my throat a stone

STRANGE HOSTAGES

in memory of Georg Heym

Books propose liberal solutions on their shelf
But a man is drowning outside in the canal

And another man he is unable to save
And sky's uncomforting wind scours ice over both of them

And they hide from it equally inside a slippery death
That as far as they can tell is not different from very cold water

As Time is nothing but everything that is no longer here.
I want to know how men can drown and books be on the shelf

Or books get tossed into the fire and men go on living.
What are we doing with ourselves?

We have put everything on line and nothing is there.
We have lost everything and the pot is still on the stove.

The crow is huddled cold on the creaking bare branch
And the books go on for miles along the dusty shelf

Waiting for a man with no fingerprints
To read them with closed eyes.

MATTER'S SHADOW

To arm against
the adversity that comes
by thinking the wrong way

               by blaming what happens,
         by wanting what is not at hand.
Only the at-hand is the case —
       the rest is Cibola — how
to deal with the onion-domes and golden rooves
of the imagined city,
         the unfound,
            the thing that rises
      up inside
      to be believed,
to be wanted
      more than the love of this place, this hand,

when what is in-mind
      is also what is the case.

What is the relation between what is at hand and what is
      in mind?
Are they both the case
and if so is it the same case?

So I said to the beaver
      Build me a dam
Where will I get the
      water he said
or who, who will tell
      water what to do?

Water will come from inside me
      be thick and moonbeam and bile.

You don't need a dam you need
        a sluicegate he said,
go to my cousin the Knife
        or my mother the Wolf

and they'll let you out of yourself
        faster than Frenchmen talk
I heard them once in Canada
when I was making milk
        of my own beneath a sad moon
all the strange languages
        coming to confuse the silent trees,

so I said to the Knife
let my images come out

and the Knife said Already
        they are walking down the hall
opening the door,
        the door's still made of wood,
they're coming out and walking up the street
        in sun in snow
their cute white boots their bikinis their fur hats
their motorbikes and knitting frames,
        their loaves of bread,

I carved the world for you yesterday
        following your instructions
        carefully and artfully
have you forgotten my edge already,

the way you can see your eyes in the side of my blade?

So I said to the Wolf
Madame what do I want

You want to forget what you remember
you want to make love to what you think
you want to touch what you see
you want to see what you hear

these confusions are what wolves call Art
and praise the Lady they do not need
such delicate epistemologies as these
to make their wild dinners,

                              a wolf is modesty,
                     pasta with broccoli or a little sheep,
a glass of time,
                     a cheap reprint of some classic text
to prop against the moon and read
                     softly out loud while the clouds scud past

and there was the moon again so I asked the moon
and listened while she said

but got distracted by her beauty
the way the lustrous curve suffused some cloud
          snow clouds on the march from Canada in fact

suffused them with the light of form,
                    and form is the Great Seducer,
          teasing light down into matter,
                         until all we think and feel is just weather,

but this is what I think she said
          Listen to my light

          my sky is bare
          to accommodate
          the ravings of your silence

I am ready for your testimony
come, write it on my hand
        the way a schoolgirl writes down a number
so that later she, so I
        can call the world
and tell everybody what you think you mean
she said.

Oneonta

THE BIRD BECOMES
THE VICTIM OF THE EYE

after the Albanian poet Mirko Gashi

Where are you taking
me to be a bird
that you're beating
so hard with your sky

the sad air that is all
we know of heaven
tortures us with feelings
— who needs those

they twist us out of the air
I need you I think
I can't stop thinking
about you ever

the terrible river of circumstance
icicles hang from my roof
and still I think I need you.
But who needs thinking?

THE EXILE

you should have seen the sun where I come from
and roads deep in winter mud
and the dirt red and black and wet

you should have seen the lakes we had
wide and flat and quiet in the sunshine
and our nights were dark
and the stars were points of light
alive with movement

and our trees with ever-widening reach
greened the whole sky and we stood beneath them
on rainy days and felt the soft rough bark
against our naked backs

o the skin we had and the grass and the roads,
you should have seen the wood we had,
you should have seen our stone
you should have seen our skin

and the moon we had
you wouldn't believe it
and the hills were high,
the moon sat right over one
yellow and big, mottled
blue a little as if we bruised her with our eyes.

EMERGENCY

It was one of those moments
when I couldn't be sure if what I felt
was physical or mental.

White moments
          a pale intensity. A ringing
absence.

          It was like the memory of a smell
without the smell,
                    a big hollow place inside me
dangerous, like a whole new day.

I seemed to have been here once or twice before.
And knew nothing.

Only that my fingers felt longer
as if they were trying to escape from my hand.

BIBLIOTHÈQUE IRRATIONALE

Write a list here of the books you've always wanted to read
and divide the result by all the ones you know the names of
but wouldn't read on a dare, like *Vanity Fair* or *Stella
Dallas*. The quotient (is that the word I mean?)
is the library of which I speak, the mysterious never-ending
alleyways of Geist down which feral pussies stroll
and you go with them, always waiting one last turn of the
tale. Meow. It is a breaking (that's what fraction means)
that has no smooth edges, a series that comes to no clear end.
There is always a hero with one foot over the cliff,
a heroine who Has to Choose, a villain with his pants on fire.
But nothing comes of them, ever, except more going.
Eventually death makes its ridiculous arrangements
and one more love won't answer the phone.
                                               Eventually
I suppose even I won't be around to keep the tally
of all the beautiful destinations even the sleaziest
departures can somehow be summoned to control.
But till then I flourish beneath the palm trees of Santa Monica
digging down into the square root of Book. And there you are.

NAUSICAA

From the raft
of all his instances

half-submerged
wallows inshore

she stumbles
towards it

comes out in surf
to guide it home

to her vocabulary
land this wood this salt

this dying man
she notices to life again

slowly
the way the sundial

swoons into evening
he comes

with his history his wives his
bronze mistakes

it will almost kill her
to decode

she survives
the way a wound does

a change left
on the face of things

a philosophy
a scar.

GARY GAETTI RETIRES

Recentior DH Red Soxorum carved on his plinth.
Is there a message in this? He did it with his nose,
profile, *figure*. The animal with the red stockings
who had long before been Gemini. Things change.
If they stayed the same where would I be? Avenue
S and Gerritsen Avenue, Sheepshead Bay by night
and a pillar of salt by day.
                              I will not look back.
Baseball plays me all night long, the situation.

Brave mothers who send their sons to school.
The yellow leaves and so on, the school books
conventionally strapped together with a belt.
Whose belt? Whose pants are falling down
and everyone pretends to laugh but secretly
comes alive with inexpressible desire, The Rights
of Man.
          Memorize them. The right to smoke
with passion when sun nibbles on the morning lake.
(In the spring sedges, multiple blackbirds
church it hard.) The right to hear you, sugar
maple. (The karaoke of the wind I keep trying
to make sense of.) The right to hear everything as words.

The right to forget what you were about to do
and have to go back into the kitchen to remember.
It all starts with forgetting, anyhow. Forget this.
A man you never knew is leaving town. A hand
you never touched has switched off the light.

PRIVATE EYE

Evidence all points to Texas, which he pronounced
in what he took to be the Spanish fashion,
clearing his throat in the middle of the word.

There is an anecdote like this in the *Aeneid*
isn't there too, which he pronounced in the old
British fashion, with stress on the first syllable,
hoofmarks shambling backwards through the slime.

Mud month in the northern earth, which somehow
he made to sound like home, horses thundering
over the dry hill in a Hollywood cloud of dust,

which he pronounced like the billowing steam
that stifles the back room where the dry cleaner
finishes a pair of my pants on the pressing machine.

I saw one die once on an August day, next door
to the butcher shop, so that veal scallopine ever
after looked like the grey face of the heart attack

weltering on the sidewalk indifferent to the ambulance
so preposterously slow in coming, which he pronounced
like Brooklyn, like a bird flying out of a bush,

thus like an old woman cautiously watering her daffodils.

THEOLOGY OF MIND

When I say mind, I mean desire. When I say desire, I mean you. When I say you, I mean your skin. When I say your skin, I mean the way in. When I say the way in, I mean the way into the dark. When I say the dark, I mean the place where there is listening. When I say listening, I mean listening to the word. When I say the word, I mean a bone. And when I say bone, I mean the ocean, but when I say ocean I mean a book. And when I say book, I mean the law. When I say law, I mean tethers and fetters. When I say fetters, I mean a knife. When I say knife, I mean wisdom. When I say wisdom, I mean your body. And when I say your body, I mean your mind.

STUNT MAN

It never happened. All those miracles
you think you saw,
fish, lepers, crucifixion,

jamais, the long amazement
we both live in still.
I was a master of seeming

and seem so still. Docetists teach
that I only appear,
a pellicule on film, an image

that made you think a man is dying
in the heart and hurt
of ordinary life. Their heresy

is all that's left of me.

MONTREUX

As if all of Europe were just shitty music
and your sleek skin.
                              But at evening
when the jasmine blooms
and the white smell
so deathly gorgeous mingles with the lake,
with the aroma of the döner kebab
peddled in the shadowy palmettos
but still is jessamine,

a fragrance that is a radiance —
I have seen the luminous banisters
leading skyward to a decision
that is the condition of someone
sitting back to back with love and facing the music,

Switzerland, *je vous assure*, is the tristest Tropique.

The flower, the immense
scent of it, the unending under of it,
billowing up out of the night,
flooding the scant remaining life

and evening when they open
white out of abysses of white.

IN MEMORY OF VENABLE HERNDON

Once again only the whipping of flags at night
—Breton

I have lost so many
to the argument of death
his seedy logic
disarms the world.

Hektor, spit on the dust
so that some trace of you
will last

      bluer than this uncertain
heraldry
      undone by what perfects it,
the moon, rising.

IN FLIGHT

Giving you grief then remembering you
were only nineteen you said though the cup
was full already and we'd been over Africa
when the flight was diverted to Dubai.

There is always somewhere else to be.
You wanted to be with your girlfriend
you called her and I asked her name
the way one does and you just smiled.

I thought you were maybe your own girl
a secret cloud-dweller lived from you
and gave you everything you could dream up
but bore no calendar of bone no skin

to wrinkle or forget. Down there the Delta
of the Nile you looked across my shoulders
and saw colors fingering each other. The sea.
Every man is Osiris. We all die. Women

look for us till they die too and this
is called the wisdom of the world. We yawned
at the same time. Rainbow over our port wing
amazing in the legalistic desert light

and you told me you believed in God.
I wanted to ask Which God and What Name
but knew I'd only get the same sad
little smile. God too you carried inside you

and all at once I burst out and asked you
then why on earth do you travel at all
when every love and every fact is stored inside.
I'm not going anywhere you said. Are you?

SEEING

Reading, the eye goes right to the most dangerous word, where the heart's obsession stores its foul locker-room gear and never throws anything away. Never thinks anything *for the last time*. What we see, we see forever.

The eye knows, that traitor Dante called it, that wants to look and look no matter how it wears itself out in looking, and then in weeping, weeping, the eternal separation of itself, himself, from what he saw. What I saw. The sickness of what we think about too long.

But the ancient Jews bent their heads forward between their knees and wept, wept until a room lit up inside them, wept until they saw. And saw for the first time what they had read and heard about but never seen. Weep, they tell us, hold your head down between your knees and blur your eyes with tears until you really see.

In the dark house of my childhood
the only escape was touching things, and things
were allies then, to cut free
from the meanings the old ones wanted

into the meanings of the things themselves,
the way they let me touch them and be wrong.
Walk in the backyard and pray to the garage,
its tar-paper roof dripping with dingy snow.

A rough stone wall was God enough for me then,
and a dirty window you still could see through.
A thousand years ahead I glimpse your face
looking up from something you are reading.

ISLAND

Sweet peas along the beach: beach pea
mauve-flowered, a quiet morning
and my brain won't work

fascist powers that hug the coast of thought
lust annoyance satire fear
turn all perception into sitcom
the sun is always close behind the cloud.

Sometimes the names of things form
a catalogue of reproaches
and it's hard to think of a word I haven't failed

every word is a guilt and a confession
every name is someone I betrayed

and this ocean out there beyond the sandpipers
past the turbulent sea roses how have I
failed it most
                    by silence or by so easily
including it in my discourses
as if I had a right to The Sea.

IN THE CITY OF HANNOVER,
BIRTHPLACE OF KURT SCHWITTERS

Ordnung gegen Ordnung

In so beautifully ruly a place
any thrust to disturb
or make wild things happen
must itself arise from orderly
principles, weighty thinking.
Dada. Oulipo. You
can't just break a glass,

       a glass

needs a reason for shattering
more persuasive than Newtonian
physics, impact, pain.

Flowers are no different,
everybody has a theory,

colors, colors —

look at the pansies, for Christ's sake,
metaphors, puns
and scribbling with chalk all over the sidewalk.

Words try one at a time to recover
the silence they abrogate

and we try to abrogate words by writing them down

so I am writing an ode called *?O*
the sound of the mouth before speaking.

OLYMPIC HYMN

O if that one over there could be under here,
The woman in the window in the rain.

Old man you saw her, you tell the story.
The rest of us were watching the runners

And you watched her
You watched her make sense of the window

And reach through it, her bare arms
Reaching out to the rain

As if it were something she could know
Something she could bring into herself

While we were watching television, we
Were leagues away and watching

Watching, but you saw.
Old man, tell us what you saw

When it was night and the woman,
Not specially young and certainly not old,

With bare arms, dressed in a simple
Dress, blue maybe, her hair dark

By color (or was it just the night?)
When she reached out into the rain,

What did you see? What do you think
Even now, thousands of years later,

The next morning, she really wanted,
Really reached for? Some gold

160

Experience hidden in the night?
We watched swimmers and riders, leapers

And fallers, we saw the young exult
Like nasty brutes, we saw them cry,

Sportured animals trapped in striving,
We watched and thrilled and mourned

But you saw. Did you see enough
To know what she was thinking?

We have watched everything won and lost
And picked up and forgotten, and now we know

There is nothing in the world worth knowing
Except what someone else is thinking.

Do you think you know what she was thinking?

PIETÀ

They took him down from his cross
But by then it was too late.
He had seen something from up there
That would not let him live.

They poured wine in his hurt mouth
And stuffed bread between his teeth
But he shook his head and would not eat
Because I have seen what I have seen.

THE TIGHT-ROPE WALKER

an appropriation-defilement of Mallarmé's great sonnet

The sea lens all ready, freedom's desperado
With more than a simple leap upon the rope
Watches his footsteps' imminent collapse
Down marbled surf with not much meaning.

Over triumphant granaries he spills
Hieroglyphics of exultant wheat
Spelt in winged grains of his fatal meat
To coax the armoire of the sky to open

And let out bird or ordinary cat or flower
In master mummery of some human season
Born in the sexy squalor of that dream

Golden witches pray to their dull god.
For dream is liturgy — and this the holy moon
Ill-silenced by the dawn itself will prophesy.

THE SECRET COURT

"Have you ever noticed how a criminal
smiles like a cello? How the moon
sneaks up through the raspberry bushes one night
and over gorse another? What shall we
do with time?"

        (Isn't number
itself the crime?)

        "Have you ever
tasted heather?

        fetal heartbeat measured
on the pulse of a deer stretched
over the chasm
between one person and another
leaping,
        foreleg there and hind leg here,
the world's retreating, have you?"

(My lawyer rises to resist.

"Linenfold wainscot, neatsfoot oil,
  egg of plover!"

        I almost believe him.
I am guilty and I know it,

        I confess
I want you, I dream of the occasion,
how could I refute the accusation?)

"This man (he turns to me) is Mercury,
how could he help but turn
her Gold into his bleak alloy?

Tarnish is his native language,
yet how bright!"

        (Almost believe him.
The jury's eyes are weeping,
I am guilty of their feeling,
              Drumbeat,
snug black skirt, tie pin, pleading,
guilty of being what I am,
            of wanting
the one thing in the world I'm not,

easy now, pastoral, lento, I mean you.)

"Let no man outlive his muses, no
mercy, the court is sleeping."

I throw myself on their imagination
as if a bird without a feather flew
down the sea sky and transcended
the simple earth on which it might have landed.

THE TORSE OF ANIMA

I have married a map and come up fire
cracking tower mute petroleum
a stupid metaphor rules the world
the dust storm turbine devil letters

print the name of your love in every shadow
old fashioned as blue *ars combinatoria*
a classroom dithered by the giggles cause
every word is funny if you look inside

since this was Africa before the ocean came
arguing our chromosomes apart rosettes
for leopards blue eyes for Picardy terebinth
in deserts organic solvents sunrise

so hot the living day bring peace on ceremony
lack is lord of want and has but yearning
pay by yen the longest ocean timothies the shore
by dint of urban values grass towers one

no longer is the same as all I seek to penetrate
the shimmer salty womb they call the future
a man coming through the gate to sell an ear of corn
is me at your knees I am your father too

no person can make do with less than three
the one who made you the one who found you
and the one you spend your life researching
until the trinity is done and you are you at last

your own son and the holy breeze churns in
from the Atlantic fog we grew up worshipping
steadfast and hurricane and wordy rock
the shingle pebbles are such unlikely flowers

musk over ambergris a bullkelp testicle
to reek in rock pools live long enough for indigo
each age a segment of the spectrum reach
under me and beyond the other all your sex

transposed magenta a daring field to kill
or bring to live by color alone! the rapist
of colors the metropolitan of smells a priest
is a priest in any skirt Nijinski's anniversary

for I too wanted to leap up with my haunch as yare
as a négresse by Baudelaire constrained to fly
when all I wanted was the Torse of Anima the skin
of theory and the meat of someone actually being there

desire being apt to this misprision to think is real
and real is inconceivable I break my candle short
and burn it in any apse because cathedrals'
rear walls curve and amplify the virgin light

into accesses of orgasmic blue lady-chapel full of go
I stayed and sympathized like an aunt with shingles
praying to you every moment on my beads of horn to come
relieve me from my silence when that! alone

was your princeliest gift a dewdrop from your tongue
a round ripe silence smithied by your womb
then loined into me by the deeds of grace you oil my lips
you nipped my tongue so that it would not tell

the actual enterprise of being still out loud
and very fast because my shabby bathrobe on the subway
sea fogs and chanticleer and Vatican and lust
and all your oil could barely wet my skin

every history is antipodes the deserts of opera
blue dye comes off your jeans and stains your thigh
because my mother was a druid and all women still
the gift of giving answer most immaculate sin

great city big enough for every love the tower
every is and every word a pinnacle researched
a sentence is a city is a man she is
because every word is vortex beating in

and forward through the sentence and up to god
that dialect of sky no one can speak
and every body imitates we are veined in water
veniced with sumptuous departures come

everything tells you to be a boat this mundane
gondolier beneath the skankiest rialtos offers you
for a bridge is a boat's dream of heaven to be
here and there at once in one great prance over hydrogen

because it does not stop and all its forms are licit
bare locust tree with a hawk sitting in it waiting
or is it watching or in museums as we stand
staring at the wall really looking for prey

waiting for the fatal move in art that makes it ours
the fatuous Teotihuacans of Republican politics
sell everything then buy it back again forever
till only one of you has all my money then

strolling through the gutted dream fish scale bright
architectured sheen in atmospheric nitrogen
winter stumbling among the ghost of Penn Station
still shimmer-teaching Room and Scale and Balance

all round the ruin of its grand proportions
the city body grows its beauty still flesh of light
round riverruns of stone and all that stays
is the grief of an idea fixed smile of a thought

fallen asleep amid thinking and stale no good to us
but the ghost is good not what we remember
but how the building stood and by itself projected
arrogant destinies we could marry could inhabit

basements in the sky profound as typewriters steeples
lead-roofed like Loire chateaux but who dares speak
geometry now when all the fashion is arithmetic
silly add-ons of unpersoned marketeers

outside the buses knew the one thing I wanted most to go
north was clarity past the tiny elegant boutiques
where we bought and cry identity outside to
the shapely ear into which this word that is the city speaks

and live there with a thousand pencils to build on rock
a magnate of meaning in an unparsed land
forest once and forest again and I'm the little light between
to be a house at last is only to give pleasure.

I lick my knuckle and taste my blood.
This little wound is cosmology enough.

Look, I have a body, I have a hand,
I have skin and something can happen to me,

A wound proves I'm actually here,
Actually alone in a world full of solitudes,

A hermit in a forest of absolutes,
And the music, for Christ's sake, the music

Comes from before I was born, the tender
Beauty that just seems to mean old, old, old,

And then I get born and inherit my silence.
So the taste of blood in my mouth

Is the same as a word,
Language the first and last of all our wounds.

POLITICAL POEM

And the spongy light was all about us,

waiting for a new catastrophe
here among the civil particulars of supper

the spongy light
blurs all the edges

we sink
into radiance

dreamers. Dreamer,
how dare you touch me,

your soft cheek
trying to own me
out of the drunken archive
where our images tumble

in vomit and patchouli
spilled stars riot

then Alan Gilbert says, and I love this,

"just be grateful the falcon has been fed"

for things rise up from us
and soar
above the common hungers

and best for us indeed
when they do their hunting and their feeding
in what passes for our dreams

and we wake
to find the bird is sated and wise

the way you wake
to find yourself embedded
in the night you left

(the thing I miss about alcohol
is the morning after

and still the lovely sand-eyed bleary dawnlight
remembers itself in me)

and the sun rises
like a thousand
bleeding harps

                Kristin Prevallet says we can hear.

But eternally sober
I have to stagger
to the writing desk
out of some renaissance comedy

to scribble my message to the galaxy

but the dying man "drank all my ink
thinking it was medicine"
                    the monk in Herzog says.

Nothing to write with
but other people's words

and that is the delicate
dishonesty
that makes us true,

the sensual honesty
of "our hybridity"

to live in their language
the way mitochondria
live in us.

How old were you when you were born?

UNIFYING THE ESSENCE

The wine they give us, the furniture in the room.
As if we bring nothing with us. Just the mean
Little eyes we notice with, he said, we stand
For nothing in particular, we stand around instead.

Is that an epigram? I said. He said, An epigram
Is a kind of instant boredom, something
Offensively the case.
                          I lost you, I said, and he,
Helping himself to more baked brie, observed
That girl against the curtains looks like my third wife.
Fine boned women are ambitious, I remembered,
Ain't that just the truth he said and slipped away.

At last this little piece of string
looped around a girl's wrist saying
remember to love this man
more than the other, because a string
makes a knot only when you stress it
that otherwise is so loosely slung
lovers lying together easy in the sand of the bed

is a piece of string. A mystery
like a church on fire I saw from the window
reaching past the blue and white porcelain
Chinese urn full of blue hydrangeas

to see actual flames. A string is like a fire.
Like water. "When the fire comes   *Noble Drew Ali,*
I will be water," the martyred Imam said,   *ca. 1926*

because things blossom in the bosom of each other.
I heard that in French once

as a bus full of women in woolen skirts sailed over the hill.

SEA MIST

So long they were away from people on their island their fogs our
fingers trying to understand one another's faces no moon in that
sky no stars beneath such clouds or maybe this really is the surface
of stars what they're actually like this gloom is Sirius and I cannot
find you

maybe this is what the stars really are and all their famous light
comes only from the friction of hot distances alone

and each star by itself is mute and netherlandish with grisaille a
street of hopes and houses left abandoned in an endless early winter
where in the howl of wind we make believe we hear geese and wolves
and gulls yammering at the industrious sea

and fog like this makes every priest an atheist to find by touch what
he had lost in thinking.

TOTENTANZ

after an engraving of the Dance of Death, by Katherine Fryer

And Death one day came along the road I had to use. There he was, swinging his familiar scythe with what looked, and this was new to me, a stiff but still flexible handle — snathe is I think the proper name for it.

Hmm, I said, that's a surprise, I always thought it was wood.

No, he said, it's bone, backbone, in fact.

Dare I ask whose bone you use to swing that blade?

Of course. It's yours. I slay you only with what gives life. Just as your mother gave you birth, I give you death. You might call me the mother of the dark. Your Greeks ...

I interrupted: I have no Greeks.

Your Greeks, he went on, thought the spinal fluid, the fluid round the brain, the synovial fluid round the knees, the seminal flow of men, all these they thought were the same humor, *aion*, the water of life. It was the Water of the Styx, on which they swore unbreakable oaths.

No oath is unbreakable, I said.

O no? said he, and started dancing

Round me a stick
It seemed shoved
Between my ankles
And flipped me

But I danced back
And would not fall
I didn't spend
So many years drunk

Only to fall down
Now sober
Not I, not I
And so I danced

Right back in his face
More leather than bone
But still a fright
I felt his ribs

More bone than skin
And then his blade
Laid a caress
Along my flank

Where in hell
Had he come from
And what good
Did my dark blood

Do him? Can you drink
I asked him,
I can and I do
He said, but not you,

I am dancing with you
Only to establish
My right to do so
And your skill too

To stumble drunkenly
Two dead men
On a dusty road
Dancing

And all the girls
Of the village came by
Half hilarious half
Horrified to see us

We struggled half
Laughing ourselves
As if the struggle
Had meaning or goal

As if death were something
Worth doing or
Life were something
Worth losing

I tripped him
And he tripped me
We both fell down
And the girls

Helped us to our feet
Brushed me off
And one of them
Said to me Why

Were you jumping
Around in the middle
Of this old road
Old man all alone?

VITRIOL

Come with me to the enter of the earth
and see the park they said was dead

the leper trees are stammering in the dark
because the wind knows nothing but what it feels

for this was dog worth and a bland of news
this was nowhere and the mayor
spoke into the cardboard microphone
words make too much sense for such transactions

leave and believe
ora et labora monks knew how to go

enter the interior of things
because each thing is earth and each despair is natural

enter the center of each thing
and find there.

What do you find there?
You find here.

Virtue is its own reward. Pontiac and Chevrolet,
DeSoto and Plymouth, a Franciscan is coming to give sermons,
It's called a mission, it means he talks to us
Night after night until we give him money
The money we saved in little cardboard boxes
Dusky yellow boxes with slots in them
And pictures on the side of dark-skinned beings
Headed for hell unless we do something
Put a nickel or a penny in
The money gets sent to the missions

Over there in the dark countries heathen lands *the unfaithful parts*
What's most interesting is the belt he wears, a white rope
Around his middle, a hood fallen back like Barrymore
Around his neck. He has a beard and nobody wears beards
Now that Dr Wheeler's dead. Hot brown wool, white robe,
Brown beard. The stories he tells are boring,
Not about lepers and cannibals, just about churches built,
Schools started up, children christened. He makes it sound
Bad as here, boring as this church, this school, this hand
That hasn't learned how to do anything yet, anything.
Teach me to write, Father, or paint or masturbate or steal,
Stop all these sermons, Father, teach me how to do.

In these stone churches and plaster churches, Saint Fortunata
    With her new faux-marbre walls, in these bare churches
I grew old suddenly, a year is like a decade, an old man doddering
Down the aisle, seven years old, to make his first communion,
To get confirmed a lustrum later, so old, so old, my new brown
And tan two-tone sportcoat, Bonfiglio made it, a dying tailor,
Soft as cashmere, old cloth, new coat, sad amber buttons,
Sad smell of me in it and it on me, sad garments of exhaustion,

Christ, who could be more weary than a child?

Trąd was the Polish word for it, that condition early-evening
    shadows
Of ailanthus and sumac thrown on the scabby wall of old brick
    garages
When if you had any sense you were very afraid but can't say
    of what
That terrible disease called seeing or the incurable presence
    of being

Or the sickening decay of everything you wanted into what you got,
This leprosy. It is what happens to you when you touch. When you
    look up
From the book. When you look down onto the page and see
    the word.
When you run behind the scenes and touch the backsides of the
    earth.
When you breathe in the air that other people left inside the room,
The stuff called culture, music, hope. Leprosy is the remedy for art.

Ritual relinquishes control. Over simple actions
    Like a spoon. Hold me in your hand like a spoon lifted to
        your mouth.
Drink me. Now I'm beginning. This is the simple ritual called
Beginning. Wait in the dark with me until I see your light.
You are the only source. I go on scraping the potatoes,
Washing the car, writing long letters to the dead, clapping my hands.
This is the next ritual, called Waiting. Its purpose
Is to release you from the spell set on you at your birth
By the wicked enchanter named Being-Born-in-the-World.
Release you from the silence of the flesh. Please.
This is the ritual called waiting for you to talk to me,
Waiting for you to ask me a question. A certain question.
I cannot do anything till you ask. Then I also will speak.
My answer will tell us both everything we have to do.

Intricate kitchens. Down here. I invited you to my house
    So I could lick the sweat from your breasts. While you
Were busy creating a new variety of poetry, you learned it
From Lorca, you tried to sail it across the pond, it sank,
You came to me with calla lilies in your hand, saying how rank
These are, tasteless, and how common magpies are
With blue luster in long feathers we see as black. White.

You hold me tight as I hold you, we are children when it happens,
It happens to a sentence, as a sentence. Nothing else matters
But what it says in us. We obey anything spoken, we are birds,
We become any color specified, we fit inside the glove of night
And grab hold of what it and only it can grasp. Wakeless
Our little boat finds an uneasy shore. It is in my body, I swear.
"We have placed her living in the tomb!" In body deep I buried you,
You rise to me, I hear you stagger up my hallway, I feel the bronze
Of your lips brush against my neck, o these kisses of yours
Are all I know of being alive, and they slay me.

Opportunity is like a dead sun bleeding all over the dawn
So much light so little substance and now we can see everything
That fails us. The memory of my childhood no longer belongs to me,
It is general, municipal, it belongs to the street. Let Crescent have it
And celebrate with Sutter and Pine, let Cozine have it, and Conduit,
And Hale and Elderts Lane and Pitkin, let them write the scroll,
They know what happened, they know who I was and who I needed,
Streets are the diagrams that parse the sentences that spoke us
Into the world. Let them milk the moon for ink and scribble with it
All over the horsehide of the night, keep the count, tell all my names,
This is the Winter Count, it tells the names of all the ones I've slain,
Allies betrayed, loves martyred into messages, waxworks, spiny fruit
Moonshaped in the shadows, o where is love when it needs me,
        where
Does sorrow wait for us beneath the leaf and inside the loaf of bread,
All these ancient things that mean the world around us, the terrible
Contract we sign by being born, sign it in our mother's ink and never
Get that first free breath back we gasped out beneath the midwife's
        hands,
Your hands, witch of this wood. The only good reason I have to live
        is you.

Leprosy, I called my fear, face in the window, word on a page,
  Fear of the answer, fear of the hidden reason for the world.
    Pip saw God's
Foot upon the treadle of the loom but I knew he'd seen a leper's foot,
The world is worked by the agony of Someone Else, someone
        missing
In the dusty empty heart of the machine. We elect one another to
        the post,
Be my God, be the current in my vein, be the thought in my dream,
Be the dream that makes my body move and think and think it's
        only dreaming.

And in the dream an answer comes, white without ruin, night
        without dying,
Simple as a hand reaching out and a hand welcoming. To be born
        again
On the other side where the sand ends in the sea and the sea ends
        nowhere.

LIGHT

The chastity of light
is a torment to the damned

who want to sully it
with our nature

want to give it skin
and suck the skin

want to penetrate the light
force our way

into everything.
Nothing yields.

Nothing can be broken,
everything intact

and light is the skin of it.
We howl around the campfire of each fact.

WHAT YOU KNEW AS A CHILD

Imagine a teacher at the front of the room
slowly undressing

but when the clothes are gone
the body's missing too

that end of the room is empty
just sunlight, chalk dust, a new

vocabulary item on the blackboard.

TRUTH

to the memory of W. V. Quine

Bring it to the end of what else the heart desires
so subways will get there amidst amazements of the local
laity drowsing onto the express at 96th

where doors open and close on discrete magics
waking you sometimes from the torpor of being everybody
in this quickest of all cathedrals underground.

If it's not true on the subway it's not true anywhere.

AURUNCULEIA

did he say a
woman made more golden by the fall of light

dome-free, the pilgrim by the bend in the canal
where one looks suddenly at the open sea
and hears it, hears it,
                              rough slur of what the waves say,
        the girl-grain of the sea.

Quotation is the father of agriculture
we bid earth repeat
the sequences of our desires

who is this we, this abdicated fiend,
japed pinpricks of the Frontal Range,
bespoke geology. We made the world.

Red sigh some old Armenian mistakes
shrinkwrapped in patriarchal complacency,
apt to be dad, not mine, a current
pretending to be water when it
is just anxiety,
                        meet me at the well.
Bend down. Let me drink.
You come with glass.
            Everything is easy
                          when you walk there
it is the well in Samaria, I have told
you before all women the nature of my identity
or let you guess

            I'm the man who came about the language
to free it from coherence and confusion both,
free it from meaning and from meaningless.

188

Because language is a different ride,
a hunger strike against the tyrant mind,

silly fascination, nothing to eat,
a fly walking for hours on an empty plate.

ALL THROUGH THE NIGHT

Dream of and touching to instruct
gleam on car hood (the punishment)

stripped of string music no back-up alone alone
instruct her — hollow tree trunk message —
every name a melody — safe journey, honey —

outside the Temple in the Bible of course I want
do it by touch not commentary hallelujah
teach the fusillade from interrogating Eros tell ask tell
tell ask a hill in hills a stone in the stream

she's driving her black car and I want green
Luftwaffe scarf around her silken neck
the old supremacist tra-la-la

(the sun is out) (I want more money)

SECOND CHORUS

Rapt into splendor señor a restoring
calm falls on the city Cooper Union Cooper Union

honey salted cashews did you know the shells are poison
roll over on the downtown local enduerme

like a pineapple biches means gazelles

not gorillas name your values
chrome entitlements you blue blue blur car
now hurrying home Cooper Union cooper is a
kind of barrel maker and his yard is flush
with warp wood he has the knack of curving

just like the backside of your cello
to blend with others of its kind end here
the gospel preachers shouting in the vestibule

THIRD CHORUS

Landsmen meet and boil some barley
so here's my story my mommy took me from my daddy
and did whatever they do they do inside you know
it's like a butchershop a school an animal
it's like a church a shoestore a snowstorm a bingo game
and you're drunk for three or four years
then you can talk, talk enough to keep them off

distract them from your actual intentions
your center your attentions the one you mean
the one you're always getting ready for señor,
the bagpipe player who fainted on your lawn
the harpist who still was there at breakfast.

TWO DEER

*In his lecture on the bizarre, Jacques-Alain Miller
discusses the impulse to tell everything, calling
it the* tout-dire, *and says it is at the heart of
psychoanalysis while at the same time called
into question by psychoanalysis*

Of course I want to tell you the blue
Shadows the naked trees put on the snow
For their own inscrutable education
Pointing this way and that, what are they,
Alphabets? From the beginning to now.
To tell everything. All the boring exactitudes,
The predictable blushes and confusions
Too dear to risk offending by the truth
That meager locker room I keep
Charging out from to find you, a hunter
Without breakfast, a pathologist
Without a corpse, a movie theater
Without a candy stand, what can I make up
To tell you true? It is two deer
Standing in the woods. One nuzzles
Gently the rump of the other, thinking
I will adore this person, thinking if I
Were a wolf I would bite this person
But since I'm what I am I will love.
It is the only natural religion.
I wanted to tell you about my fears
As if they could touch you. The deer
Are still standing there on duty
Waiting for their metaphor to close.

THE FISHERWOMAN

The fisherwoman went out alone that day
Wasn't even dawn yet the coast was pale

But that was surf the sky was dark
The boy who goes with her was not there

Sick or romancing someone or gone home
He was not there at the little jetty

He did not raise the sail or shove the land back with his heels
She went out alone this morning

It mattered little to this young fisherwoman
Whether she was alone or together

We're always alone in the important hour
The one that's coming and she raised the sail

After she rowed out into the lagoon
And down she went along the quiet sea

To come to her hour. Things wait for us.
Even there on the empty horizon where the dark

Meets another just like itself
Something a boat is meant to find.

She did not look around her as she sailed
Did not look up. She kept her eyes

Fixed on a mirror laid flat in front of her
On a little table where her wine cup stood

A mirror that showed the stars
She steered by the stars stored in the glass

And where she went the stars were going too
But always left when she went right

And each of those heroes of the night
Stood inside out above her

Hunters and harriers no more
Because a woman when she sails alone

Is the only upright presence in the world
The rest is just a sky full of bright mistakes

That lead her to the truth
The empty place inside the ocean

From which these fish are spoken she pretends to want
Find catch and bring home squirming silver

And leaves on the dockside later for her neighbors
When she comes back home and time

Has turned into something as paltry as the day.
She takes her mirror home and hangs it up

And black it is and always will be,
A glass that knows how to show only the night.

NEED

To be so far apart from what needs me
While a spool releases silky emerald thread
You loop a loop of it on cream cheese
No one can tell the eaten from the future
To mix ribbons in with your rice, a car
Running through the vly in hip-high mud
You affirm a Calvinist principle even as
Your bed is burning below the underpass

The shunts of population dismay classicists
Stardust is actual enough the problem is harps
To hear it, Aeolian extravaganzas a priest
In Portugal praying for a cold white egg
Between the cheeks of his beloved, agree
With your impulses before they candle
And there the night is ruined with gold
Gleam upon oil a translator comes home

Mess rich with latin lipids a blue hair
Looped around your argentine hour
(Hair, hour, hour, hair, who are there
Who kiss the long triangulars of narrative
Sauntering Tiergarten one tall gold girl)
Back from the war striations of belief
Cheesing their way through dull wax
'Marble that seemed to be on fire'

Was there an answer only a humming
When the book was opened as if owls
Had recently flown past and bees remembered
Shadow governments by neat procedures
Forget everything that can be lost is lost
Kayak under trestle wooden sleeper grazes
Tall type in a canoe slug in a turnstile
Halfway to Verona there is a mountain

Too close to the trains the cosines are wrong
But the geometry of morning still works
The shadows fall the shades go up the woman
Stands at the window inspecting her reflection
Ghosting in the glass before the whole street
This is the first story in the history of things
A woman with a looking glass man with rock
The last encyclopedia is full of sand.

SUICIDE NOTE

Most nights I sleep on the other side of dream
healed in black nirvana that wakes up for breakfast
where all the people are who dream me.

Why can't I dream of what gives pleasure?
A word swells up until it hurts you need to drain
suck out the beesting venom of all history

naked naked as a text without its commentary
these antisemite animals that hate analysis
when all is solving up and going down a god
given gavel rapping in the skull to punctuate

the stupid single meanings of the world and let
them pullulate until the cows come sagely home
into the stone barn built before the universe
full of good intentions I beg you milk my book.

Exhausted porters bring my body home
green fever took me and I slept the lake
talked to me constantly using little words
so we could learn them this is water.

A name's as good as any other lie, trickery
of the moon, be brief with me I have to get
back to ruling long sheets of paper with pale feints
man proposes woman exposes cherry trees safe
at last from hares a postcard big as a burn
licks the color off your eyes and whispers thanks

on cloudless Sabbaths a new geometry of malls
rinsed clean of laughter the sky is one long ad.

ARCHEOLOGY

Past all far interpretations there are glazes and blue frits
Baskerville pushing narrow gutters to spill a wide sestina
so many things I want to pull from the chronicle of skin
to read to you amid the sunken cathedral in my anxious whisper
my whole life has no other purpose than to make you hear
the ring forts of Atlantis each one a different color piled
like quoits around the middle pillar of the world the town
inside the city in our bones, neat flesh of ours the ocean
swallows down the wisdom city we keep looking for

IDENTITY

You fucked a mirror and gave birth to me
if me I am. I mean if all this heap (to use the technical
word — sorites — to translate a no-account nihilogism
a skandha in sunlight and the wind blowing

cool as somebody else's radio always tuned to
in the know) should happen to have accumulated
like a sentence in a legal document to actual beans
from which we could be born and born again

fluttering god's own blue helter-skelter cosmogram
scaring learned penguins as they scatter with dignity
over the appalling university of ice that's all
the world finally has to offer as opposed to its opposite

whatever that might be. Water. That's all it gives us
and from this little spurt of moist we write a sprout
that springs a world out of the most unconsidered
spherical geometry of the kitsch we live among

and that world in turn lotuses out like Christmas
with its tongue on fire and says *you* for instance
until I can't bear the solitude of not saying it too
and I turn out to have been the Holy Spirit all along

and isn't that amazing whether you think so or not
that this bland blend of not much in particular
should be enough to be particular just because
there's meat on the bones and a voice in the cellar.

SIN

To write with the sin because
　　　sin has to do with being

All we have left to talk with
　　　is our sin

We all know that but don't say so

Composition is always a fall

Falling from all that could say
　　　into what one actually does say

Such a shriveling

Sin is a shriveling

In the big place where everything else in the world
　　　could be said

Only say this little place of this

What a small thing to do

So writing is small

Tea stain, no

Birthmark on the white paper

Smaller than all that could have been said

Only this gets said just now

Out of all that could have said itself

Only this

But even this little this

Brings things to mind

When you say a word twice a
        sudden mirror

A hole in the cellar wall of your house

And a whole new apartment in there

Furnished for you

Filled with whom

Writing is so small

But it brings things to mind

The furniture of all I am there for you
        say

Sin reminds

Sin reminds of other things

We always need other things

Here needs there

Virgin room
        below your house or dream

A room a new room

Sin is a new room to be in
          to be you in

A bone of being there

A collarbone to hang the veil of flesh from

The famous dance one needs the bone to do

Sin bone

Bone reminds and bone remembers

And then the dance

Happens but not easy

Never easy always simple
          do it

A comma is always in the wrong place

An interruption always is glad

A sin is glad

The task is to stain

A duty to do to you

White neck

Sun writes the page quick

So quick we can't see the pen

Only the shadow of actual words

Sin says anything that comes to mind

Sin specifies

To be anything at all is to be everything.

AT THE SARMATIAN EMBASSY

I didn't avoid the reception but I thought about it
There were moons there and foreign preachers
Coins rolling underfoot a lot of them
Bronze mostly but silver here and there
The way things spill I took a glass from a tray
But didn't drink it just watched the ballroom
Founder under dull music and killjoy to the last
Can never leave a room at all confident
I have done everything I could have done in it
So stood halfway up the curving staircase
Admiring the more agile dancers some of them
Just a swoon or two away from being in love
To use a phrase from my childhood you hear
On classic movie channels to this day or night
Grave as Walter Pidgeon biscuits for la canaille
That's me I guess and go upstairs. Mrs Organ
Was resting on the chaise beside the telescope
I would like to wake her but don't know the spell
Because hanging out with people is a riddle isn't it
And leaving a party is a fatal wound received in dream.

LAPSUS

1.

Fleurs, flares? Life
a long mishearing.

Habit of the lapse, the fortunate
let fall, the slip

that is the tongue
a sweet wet sign

virgin speaking in the dark.

2.

It is so far that they have come
to be so little a thing as me

all the masters, all the angels
of the interior the gold

beating Cellinis the pale
tortured Beethovens to be me

what a futile destination for their art
yet I can walk on that meadow with them

the grass of things
allows me in that company

sundappled a few steps behind.

3.

I was there when they invented song
radio when porcelain first broke

I was a golden adder striped across the road
a little girl must have picked me up

how cool her hands made me
as I lay about her wrists.

4.

I think it is a sunshine
after all a pronoun a naked word

impossible to say out loud
I was salt bird droppings serenade

I knew the name for it
Assume nothing said the oak tree

that made my door
no one is entitled to say prayers

Show me
the little thing inside you you call me.

5.

I must have been green
on this coast of broken eggs

the lapwing trails its feather tips
twirling wounded to lure us off

apotropaic, the hope of summer
someone not finding where she nests

we watched her seaside vaudeville
how many thousand years she's tricked us

city after city and all the while
her little birds are hidden at our feet.

THE DOCTRINE OF ENGLISH VERBS

The doctrine of English verbs tells a sad science,
a lyrical experiment in being gone.

Sing, sang, sung — doing it, did it
and now it's done. But what's to come?

I will sing. Sure. We hear that will,
future marker, and know it means I want

and we know how it is with wanting,
getting what I want. Even when my will

is bent to my desire like a man
breaking his back rowing his dull boat,

all his strength, and can't see, can't see
where he's going, we row backwards

into the dark. The doctrine
of English verbs will break your heart.

SINGLES BAR

What happens at full moon
The house stays home

All our conversations leave records in the world
These memoranda in fact comprise the world

Not thought into place talked into place
Birds review their options as they fall

Old men learn why things are as they are
Only when it's too late to change

Self-absorbed but not self-aware a monkey hunts his fleas
Shouldn't the doctor and the patient have the same kind of chair

A wheelbarrow by the outhouse to carry them home
Welfare administrators howling at the moon

Every day the same man came into the bar
We wore bright green spring onions woven into our hair

One day the caravan was late the sun was lost
Heaven depends for its order on human arrangements

All the rest of it is chaos this is a rose
Ordered into place by seeing the eyes talk

One day he said he didn't feel sincere
She brought organic carrots and sat on the lawn

It's the bar stool not the beer that makes the bar
Chair means flesh in any language and good bye.

HOLDING A STONE CALLED ANGELITE

What do I feel?
A breeze from somewhere
interrogating trees.

Go buy me a window

the door is sick
wood chips scattered by my side
as if I were of their company
and knew how to fall

whereas I rise
through the hundred-story tower of the body
they will never build again

and from the observation deck recall
the simple operation of old trees

intersected by the tiresome litany of my identity,
that is to say my journey from Reality
into a comfy sense of being someone,
someone who wins and loses, touches, lets go.

        *

Made to let go
a stone in my hand
blue grey like a city
pigeon smooth
dirty water in the harbor
beautiful as what
people really think,

easy to lose in grass, in gravel,
made of what the earth is made of
I think it will last even longer than death.

THE TEMPER

after Juan de la Cruz

1.

There must be a difference between
a flame and its fire.

        Tell me what it is,
you've been in Spain,
           you've sat beside the basin of his fountain
where *la llama de amor viva*
roared up once out of the water
heating you cooling you heating you cooling you
till you were tempered
            into a strange new power,
a new kind of flesh.

The living flame of love. Or flame of living love.
No one can be sure. It surges
from the lucid water and overwhelms you,

the way quiet people in the plaza are drenched with light.

2.

You felt it in your thighs,
          in your vocabulary.
So tell me the difference,
      the flame like a tongue
the fire like a language,
      the whole of it trying to speak
what cooks in the blood,

211

                         humid fire of the alchemists,
and why do they call it blood?

It is in language that desires are stored
our bodies take out, try on, use
to quench the moral thirst the pronouns sing

         3.

as if I were the flame and you were the fire.
Is that it,
                  something so easy, as if it could be
         a family of love,
                  or love a family matter,
the terrible bullshit cartoons of the heart?

All songs end with *corazón.*
We're still trying to invent that thing,
the square-dance, the jota, the deep one,
the demon-infested four-room bungalow inside the chest,
all parador and no mirador, *el corazón.*
There, we did it again.

         4.

So you should be my son a little while,
sit on my lap and endure my absent-minded tenderness

This flesh I made I will constrain
like King Lear spanking the cold wind.

5.

All kings are blind.
Sometimes I think I only see through you,

all flesh is made to suffer
desire, ecstasy, remorse, confusion, prayer —

the five last things. And prayer? Prayer is
that whole holy silence of the body

halfway on the road between all it ever said
and where it falls asleep.

                              Needs sleep. No road.
Hold hands. Smoky wet fire.

Travelers, we come to the dark posada
where the mountain eats the sun.

CASIDA OF MILK

Everything tries to answer the question at once
This eagerness begets a material world

You know better than I how close we are
My name is the same as yours only the letters are different

He waited for the rain to stop and is still waiting
Buñuel's film pours milk on the dairymaid's thighs

Things have an odd way of being rational
A gnat in a wise man's eye sees better than he

Beneath the fur of the acacia leaves a great tree sleeps
Everything is ready for the big moment we advertise

All moments are the same size time is a cube
Time is a lump of jet fits sweet the palm of my hand

Jet is an animal that long ago was wood
An animal is anything that makes us think

I am an animal that not so long ago was you
Curvature of light around a broken vase is whole

The answer was looking for me while I hid in the woods
The answer trickled down my back while you mopped my brow

The whole world is looking for somebody to blame
Very old people learn to do it with mirrors.

SERVICE

A chickadee almost let me touch it
so determined was it to extract
the last seed from the feeder I was determined to refill.
For Christ's sake is this a church or something,
the shifting planes of sunlight along the lawn,
the leaves, the war? An owl flies by on its way home.
I am smitten by the tyranny of birds
from whom no man can rescue the sky.

THE TAROT TRUMP CALLED
'THE HOSPITAL'

Smokestacks prick into a smoke sky
billowing black

bonesmoke bloodsmoke
the reek of money pavementing the trees

sardonic trees of hospitals
where your autumn father's dying

from far off you see it
the one-way gate

gaunt rich building on the hill
solid as a loaf of poisoned bread

smoke up, signals on the roof
wink of sunlight on the dying glass.

   2.

Does it tell a story or a place,
emblem or anecdote
something you heard in the bar or told
by your own mouth to your surprise

you are turned on by the victimage of ears
they listen so you speak

the only word worth saying
is the one you don't know

it says itself
like the meaningless chime signals in a hospital

216

listen hard till you don't understand anymore
the things you thought you knew
that's what a hospital is, a place where the words are lost,

and here you thought you were a Baudelaire,
a troubador of sin.

     3.

        Listen,
there are not two journeys,
only one

every footstep a foundering boat
I tried to translate
what the dream actually said:

Tout pas voilà naufrage.

          Wiesbaden

ROMAN ALTAR IN WIESBADEN

How lost I am
in a night of things,

things I can name.
Pressure. The no
name numbers
I can't take home.

No one can own a number.
Rule of Dada. The king
stands still, the castle moves
ar-Rukh, the tower the

elephant. We saw a camel
thick for winter
munching oats below the Roman wall

2.

and by the steps beside the overpass
an altar to Mithras, the god
yanking the bull's head back

the god killing the bull.
And next to it another stone —
here the bull is dead.

But who is that standing above him?
Is it still the god? Or is he only a god when he kills?

Mithras, the good mate,
the soldier's friend. Comrade.
Pawns in horror house marching north.

And here, after twenty-one years campaigning
Dulianus fell, something like a sergeant
he had been in all those years, those wars,
fell fighting the Chatti, the Suevi,
the Alemanni, the Americani, the Nazis, the Taliban,
so many people to fight against
until you're dead
                        and here he lies
in German land. Here he is dead.

Who is it that stands above a dead one,
animal or man? Who is an altar?

    3.

Among all these altars I wanted
to remember what the sacred meant.

Be sacred
as a sock is
wet with your own
sweat shaped
to your occasions,
the flex and fall and lift
of foot, the pressure
of it all.

When something matches something else,
matches the situation so perfectly it makes you laugh:
that is the sacred.

A pair of pants flat on the bed.
Mary talking back upside down to God.

THE HERETIC

How much could I stop and still go on
Is there a reasonable answer to a pair
Of knife-creased flannels or a house in the Hamptons?
It does seem to help, pronouncing Wal-Mart Valmáhr
As if it were a place in Proust, and anything that helps
Helps, he lamely concluded, and sat down to a patter
Of tepid yet spontaneous hawsers and chains
Slipping in the night but not slack enough to let him
Sail from Port Pagliacci on the morning tide, not yet.
It's always Friday where I come from, she said,
Her green eyes glowing in the carnival of her antique
Attractions, wonderwheel, cyclone, and Time itself
Shooting past, all that irretrievable feeling-plasma
Sloshed down the drain of the hours — hippos
Waltzed to it in Disney — watch Time with me
The most is least to be, she winks at me
And I belonged to her circus, mama, never come home.
That's what I've been trying to face up to, doctor,
I have no church to go back to, no home town,
No stake to be burned at, I left all that in a locker
And took a bus to Fresno (actual fact) when there still
Were buses. What are there now? How does anybody
Move around? And does anybody ever get there?

RESURRECTION

In Piero della Francesca's *Risen Christ*
the drapery of shroud writes a letter round the man
that keeps his modesty and lets his glory through,

that angry almost disappointed face
like a householder roused at night to challenge thieves
— by being in the flesh we have broken into his house.

We stand in our shimmering loincloths just out of sight,
trembling. What will he do? Nothing. He stares at us.
We have no right to be where we are,

but pity is easy for those who have passed through death.
There is no police he can summon, no other place
to which he could exile us, he is stuck with us here,

for lewd characters like us all his sufferings
were taken on. Were we worth it? We shiver
with self-esteem. Of course we are, we're beautiful

in our disarray, meat on our bones and gaudy dreams
cycling through our heads, he should love us, he should.
He lets us be. Presently we come to worship him.

Every minute he lets us go on living seems
like a forgiveness. Sacrament of being in the world.
The rising sun. The feel of cloth against my skin.

Robert Kelly, April 2004. Photograph © Charlotte Mandell

Born in Brooklyn in 1935, ROBERT KELLY went to a Jesuit school, CCNY, and Columbia, worked for several years as a translator of scientific material, then began a half-century of involvement with little magazines (*Chelsea Review, Trobar, Matter, Caterpillar, Conjunctions*). His first book, *Armed Descent*, was published in 1961; *Lapis* is his sixty-third. In recent years he has collaborated with artists living (Kempker, Mahlknecht) and dead (Shelley) and has written a considerable number of short stories. He is currently finishing a novel about alien abduction and gathering a collection of his essays, but his main work remains the daily practice of poetry. He teaches in the Writing Program at Bard College, and lives in the Hudson Valley with his wife, the translator Charlotte Mandell.